DISCOVERING
ILLINOIS

WILLIAM STEPIEN
IDA FISHER
JOHN LEWIS
MARY SMOOT

GIBBS·SMITH
➔P
PUBLISHER

PEREGRINE SMITH BOOKS
SALT LAKE CITY

Acknowledgments

We wish to thank the following for reviewing the manuscript for the book and offering suggestions for improvement:

Dr. Alice Jurica, Director, Bureau of Social Studies, Chicago Public Schools

Victor Tocwish, Coordinator, Bureau of Social Studies, Chicago Public Schools

Table of Contents

1. Land and Climate viii
2. The People of Illinois 14
3. The Early Years 36
4. A Time of Troubles 62
5. Growing and Changing:
   Chicago Case Study 82
6. Illinois Government 116
7. Making a Living in Illinois 134
8. Connected to the World 156
   Glossary 176
   Index 182

Maps and Charts

Glaciers in Illinois 4
Illinois in the World 6-7
Growing Seasons 9
Major Rivers & Coal Fields 11
Indian Mounds 19
Historic Indian Tribes 22
European Land Claims 25
Land Claims After 1763 45
Clark's Route 48
Northwest Territory 51
Illinois Capitals 54
Civil War States 74
Illinois Railroads, 1856 89
Branches of Government 119
State Government 123
How a Bill Becomes a Law 124
The Food Dollar, Mid-1980s 146
Workers in Illinois 150
Downtown Chicago 174
Counties and County Seats 175

CHAPTER

1

Land and Climate

Summer fun on the shore of Lake Michigan.

ILLINOIS DEPARTMENT OF TOURISM

ILLINOIS DEPARTMENT OF TOURISM

Fall comes to an Illinois farm community.

Illinois forest in spring.

Many people enjoy winter skiing in Illinois.

JOHN HAZELTON, BATAVIA, ILLINOIS

ILLINOIS DEPARTMENT OF TOURISM

Glaciers like this one helped shape the land in our state. Can you see the valley, or bowl, that has been formed by the movement of the blanket of ice over hundreds of years?

LESSON 1

The Ice Age

Many years ago the earth began to cool off. Year after year, winters grew longer and colder. Summers grew shorter and cooler. No one really knows why it became so cold. We do know it was so cold that in much of the world the snow did not melt, even in summer.

Winter after winter the snow piled higher. Near the poles and on mountains, the snow became so heavy that it was pressed into sheets of ice. These huge sheets of ice are called *glaciers*. Some of the water from the oceans also froze into glaciers.

This was the Ice Age. For hundreds of thousands of years, the earth stayed cold. The ice sheets kept growing larger and covering more of the land. Some glaciers grew to be more than a mile high.

Glaciers move very slowly over the land or through the water. They might move just a few inches or feet each year, forward or backward. As they move, glaciers pick up soil and rocks. The Ice Age glaciers dragged and pushed along tiny bits of sand and even boulders as big as a small house. The heavy ice sheets and the rocks they carried ground down the tops of mountains. They widened the valleys between mountains. Sometimes they dropped some of what they were carrying. This filled in the valleys and made the land more level.

The glaciers from the north moved toward Illinois. Each year they came closer. With them came cold winds and freezing weather. Many birds and other animals looked for warmer weather to the south. Others died.

During the Ice Age, the weather was not always the same. Just as our weather changes, the Ice Age weather was different from year to year. In some years more snow fell than melted. Then the glaciers grew. In other years, some of the ice melted.

We do not know exactly how long the Ice Age lasted. But for thousands of years the ice sheets spread south, like great, slow-moving blankets. Then the weather got warmer for a time. The southern part of the glaciers melted and left behind hills of soil and rocks. Grass grew where the ice had been. But again and again the cold returned, bringing the glaciers south.

At least four times during the Ice Age, glaciers spread across parts of Illinois. One glacier reached much further south than the others. It has been named the Illinoisan. The Illinoisan covered almost all of what is now Illinois. Only two small parts of our state were never covered by glaciers.

Each of the four ice sheets changed our state. They ground down highlands and widened or filled in valleys. They also made new hills and valleys. Finally, the last of the great ice sheets melted about 15,000 years ago. It left the surface of our state mostly flat with gently rolling hills. This is how the land in Illinois looks today.

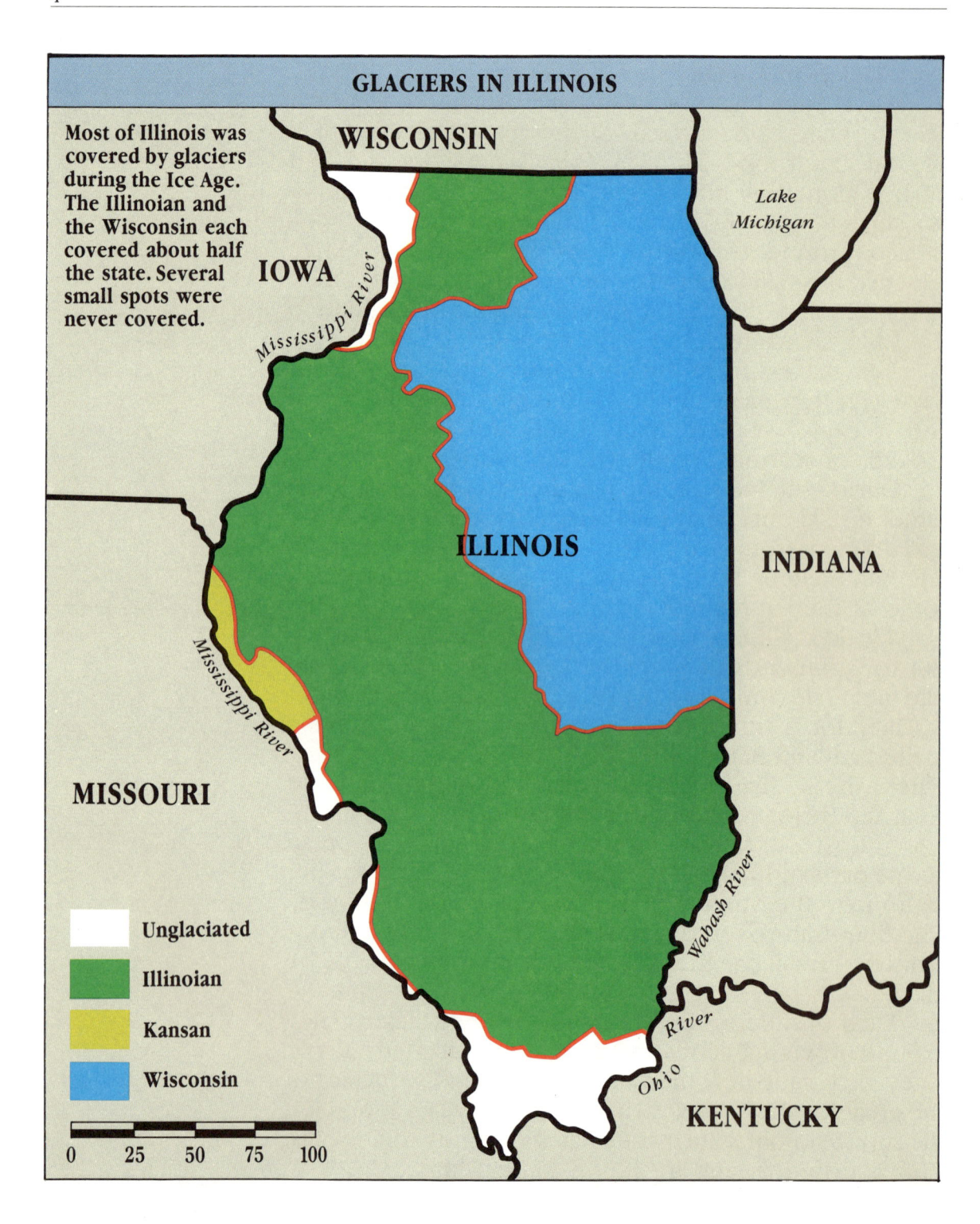

GLACIERS IN ILLINOIS

Most of Illinois was covered by glaciers during the Ice Age. The Illinoian and the Wisconsin each covered about half the state. Several small spots were never covered.

Legend:
- Unglaciated
- Illinoian
- Kansan
- Wisconsin

0 25 50 75 100

Prairie grass can still be found in Illinois.

LESSON 2

Today in Illinois

Illinois is called the *prairie* state. This nickname describes the kind of land we find in our state. A prairie is a wide, level, grassy land with few trees. Illinois is in the heart of the North American prairie. Another name for this kind of land is *grassland*.

When settlers from Europe came to Illinois, the land was covered with tall grass. Many of the early settlers moved on when they came to these grassy lands. They thought that trees did not grow here because the soil was too poor. There was little wood to build their houses. Some who stayed learned to build a new kind of house. They used squares of grass, roots, and soil which they cut from the land. They also learned that the prairies were some of the best farm land in North America.

The early settlers in Illinois found something else about our state very helpful. Over 250 streams and rivers flow through Illinois. These rivers have served the people of Illinois in many ways. First, rivers are good for providing water to farms and draining extra water from the soil. Second, rivers have been a source of water power for factories. Finally, rivers have always been an important way to move things from place to place. Even today, rivers are used to move large or heavy goods. Rivers are still the cheapest way to move large amounts of grain or oil.

Climate

Look at the world map. Find Illinois in the middle of North America. What can you tell about Illinois from this map? Illinois is in the middle *latitudes*. It is not close to the equator where it is warm all year. It is not close to either of the poles where it is cold all year. Illinois is in the *temperate zone*. It is neither hot all year nor cold all year long.

You have learned that the land in most of Illinois is level. The flat land affects the weather in Illinois. There are no large mountains to slow the wind. The wind can make quick changes in the weather. A strong wind from the south can quickly bring warm, moist air into Illinois. The wind from the north can bring

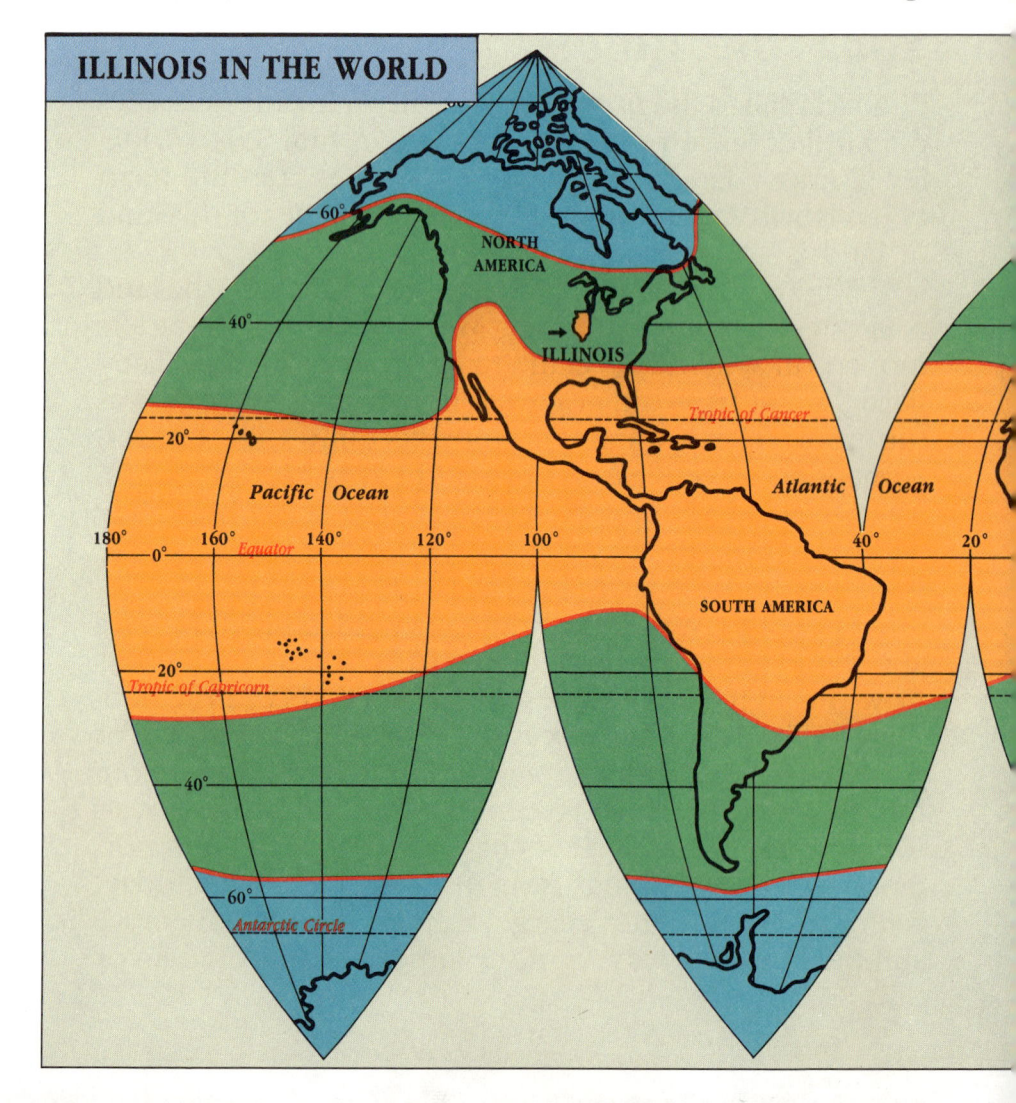

ILLINOIS IN THE WORLD

cold, dry air.

Look at the map again. Notice that Illinois is far from any ocean. Distance from the oceans also helps determine the kind of weather we have. Large bodies of water, such as big lakes or oceans, change temperature more slowly than air does. In winter the warmer body of water keeps the land nearby warmer. In summer the cool body of water tends to keep the land close by cooler.

Places that are not near a large body of water have more *extreme* temperatures than places near water. That means such places have hotter summers and colder winters. Illinois is not near an ocean. Illinois has hot summers and cold winters. One part of Illinois is near a large body of water. How do you think this affects the climate in Chicago?

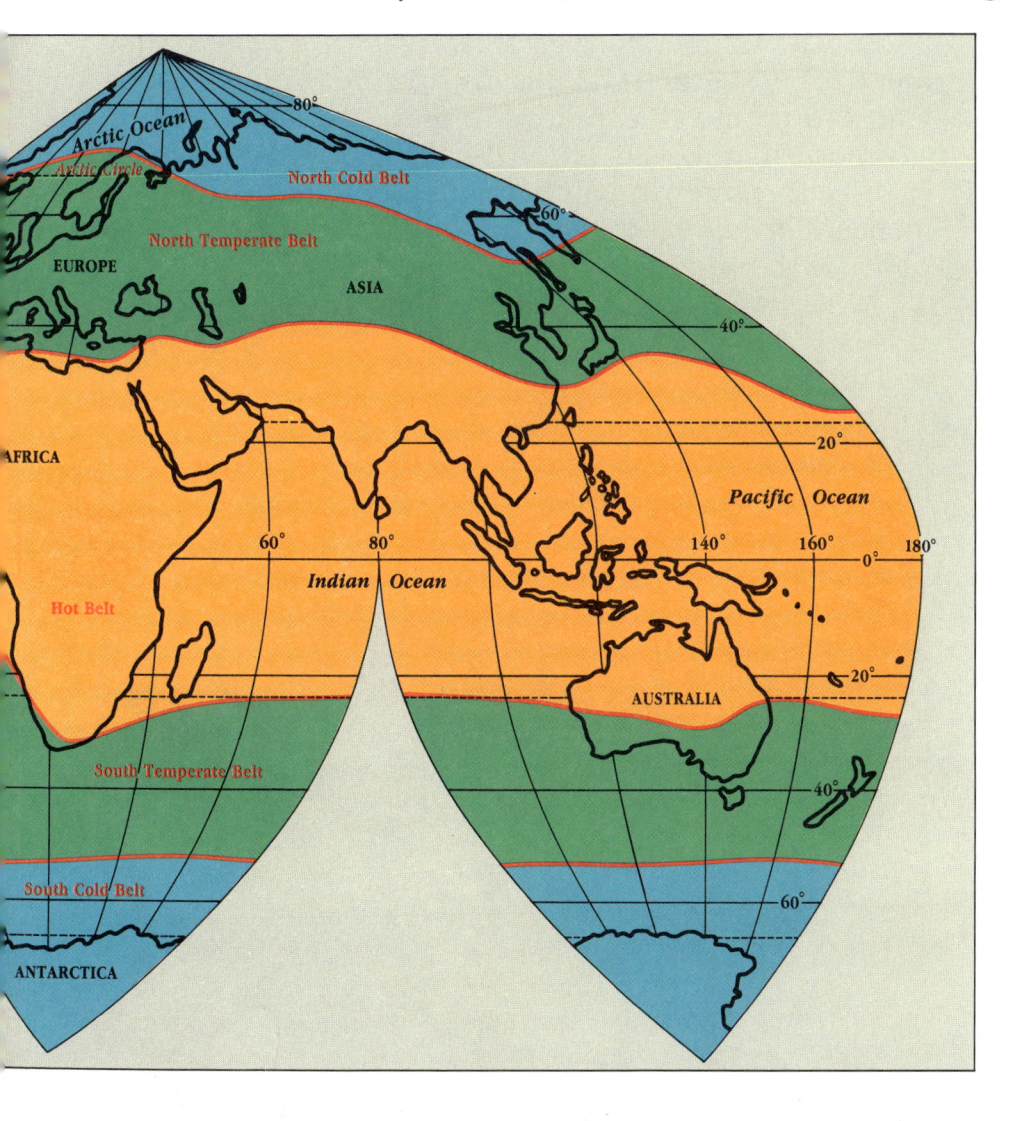

BATHTUB EXPERIMENT

Try this experiment before you take a bath. Hold your hand inside the tub above the warm bath water. Is the air above the water warmer than the air in the rest of the room? Now run some cold water into the sink. Hold your hand above this water. How does the air just above the cold water feel? In the same way, an ocean or large lake warms or cools the air in places nearby.

Illinois is 385 miles long and 218 miles wide. Because our state is so long, summers are cooler in the north than in the south. Temperature can reach 105 degrees on summer days in southern Illinois. During the winter, temperatures in the north can drop to 35 degrees below zero. Northern Illinois gets about 34 inches of *precipitation* each year. Places in southern Illinois receive about 41 inches. The rainfall during the spring and summer is just right for growing corn, wheat, and soybeans.

Now look at the growing season map. The growing season is the time between the last killing frost in spring and the first killing frost in fall. It is the time when crops can be grown without danger of being killed by freezing weather. How long is the growing season in northern Illinois? Compare the growing season in Chicago to that in other parts of Illinois. Were you right about what Lake Michigan does to Chicago's climate?

Chicago's summer weather is ideal for riding bikes.

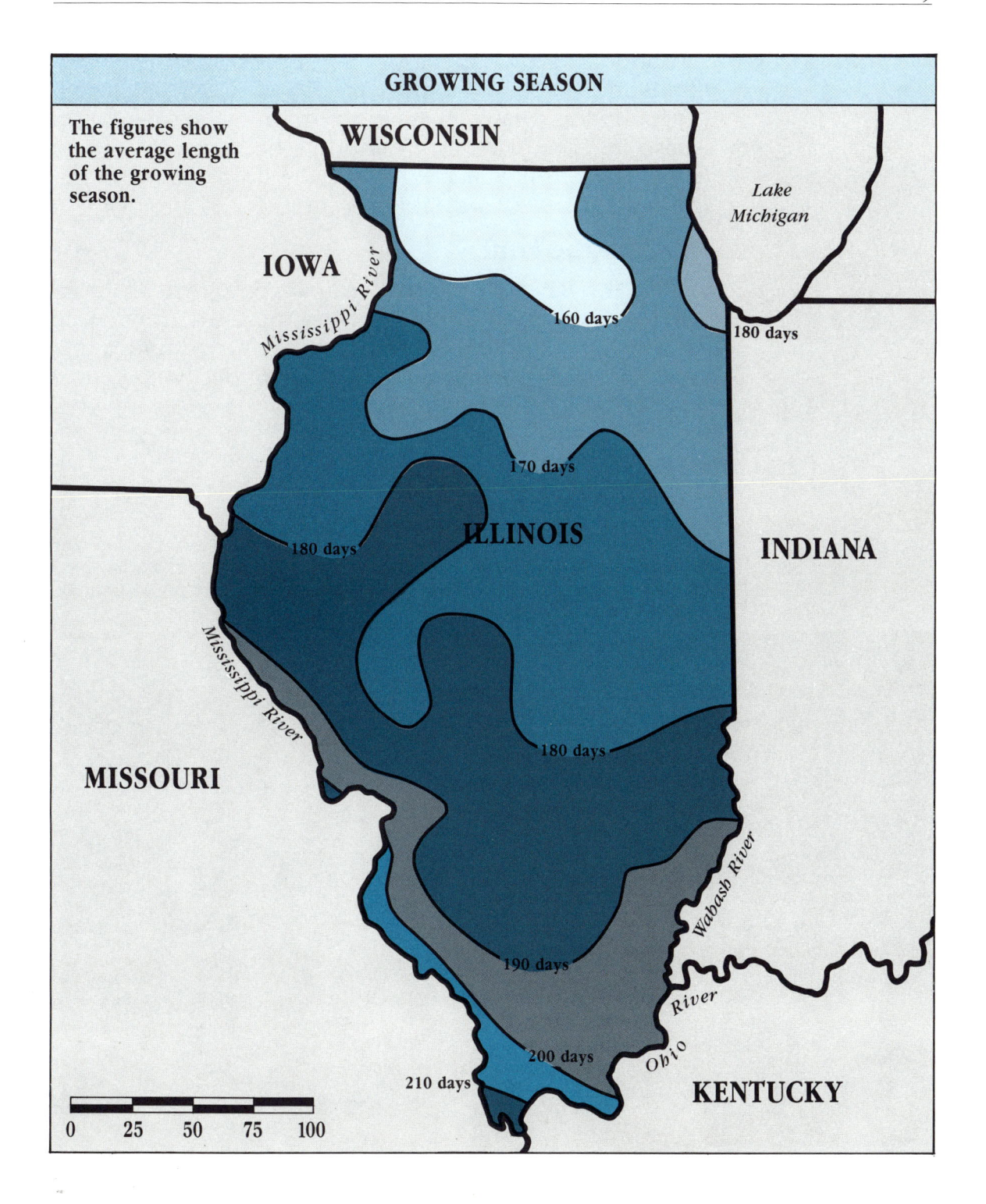

GROWING SEASON

The figures show the average length of the growing season.

- 160 days
- 180 days
- 170 days
- 180 days
- 180 days
- 190 days
- 200 days
- 210 days

Wisconsin · Iowa · Lake Michigan · Mississippi River · Illinois · Indiana · Missouri · Wabash River · Ohio River · Kentucky

Scale: 0, 25, 50, 75, 100

Illinois' growing season is long enough for most grains and vegetables. Our state has rich soil for growing crops. Illinois' many rivers keep the soil well drained. It is also an easy place to grow crops because the land is level. These things make Illinois a good place for farming. *Agribusiness* is the biggest industry in Illinois.

Beneath the land

Before the Ice Age, Illinois was part of a great tropical sea. Many different kinds of plants and trees grew here. These plants and trees died and were buried under the great sea. Over the ages, these layers of decaying plants were pressed into *coal*. The greater the pressure, the harder the coal became. Such a large amount of coal was formed that this period is called the Coal Age. The coal

This diorama at the Field Museum of Natural History shows what Illinois looked like before the Ice Age. How have these plants helped us in the past 150 years?

MAJOR RIVERS AND COAL FIELDS

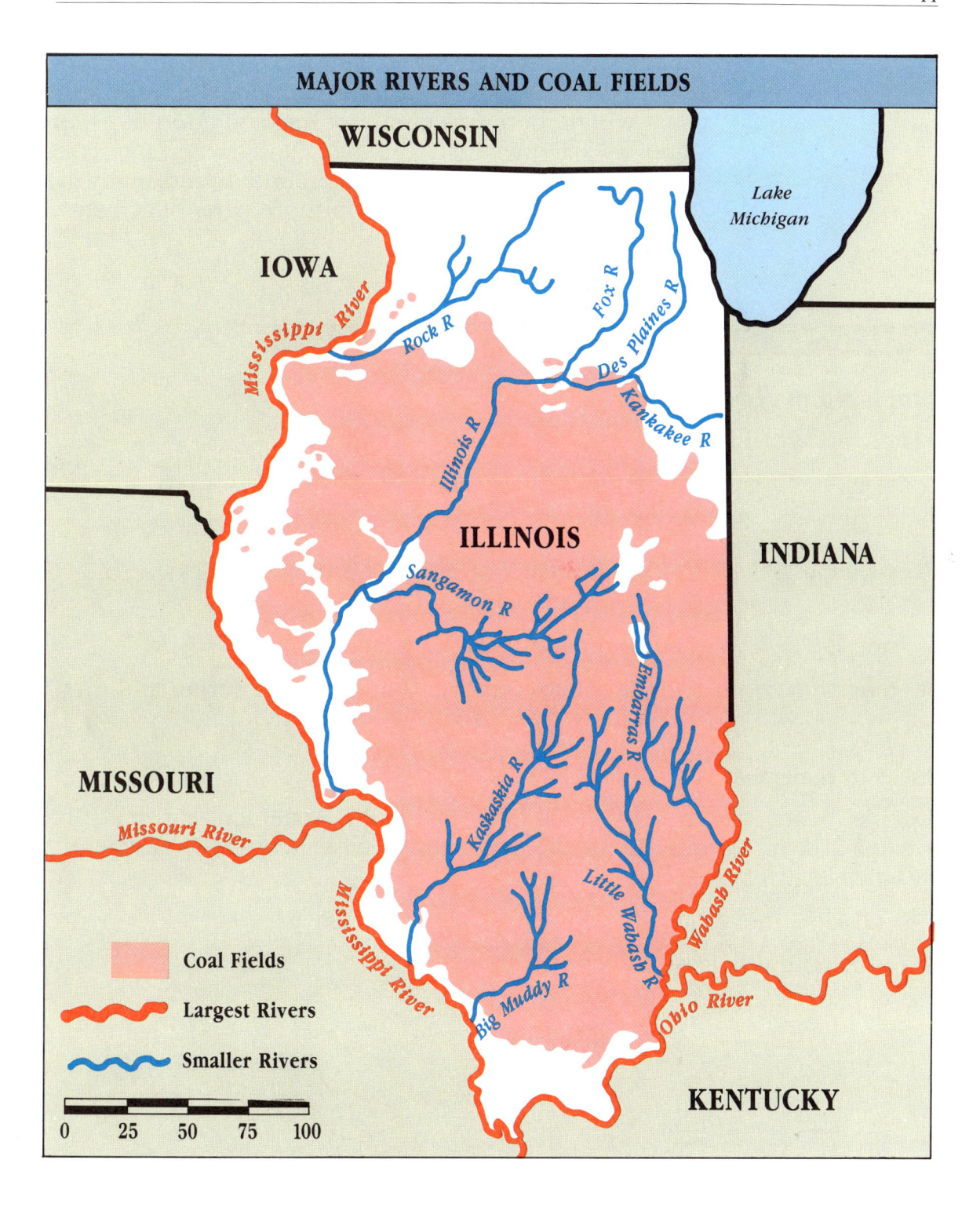

under almost two-thirds of Illinois has been very important to the growth of industry in our state. Factories were built where there was plenty of fuel and good transportation. Coal provided the fuel, and rivers and lakes provided transportation. Later, railroads and highways allowed factories to be built in more parts of our state.

DO YOU REMEMBER?

Words worth remembering

Match the word from the chapter with its meaning.

1. glaciers
2. coal
3. growing season
4. prairie
5. temperate zone

A. a wide, level, grassy land with few trees
B. neither hot all year, nor cold all year
C. huge sheets of ice which dragged rocks across the land
D. a mineral used for heat
E. time between last killing frost in spring and first killing frost in fall

Ideas to remember

Decide if each statement is TRUE or FALSE. If the statement is true, write TRUE on your paper. If the statement is false, write the statement again so that it is true.

6. Glaciers move quickly.
7. Coal is the biggest industry in Illinois.
8. Early settlers made houses out of sod.

9. Rivers are the cheapest way to move large amounts of grain.
10. Illinois has no mountains to stop the wind.
11. One Illinois city next to a large body of water is Rockford.
12. Illinois was once part of a tropical sea.
13. Most prairie land is covered with trees.
14. The time when the Earth stayed cold all year round was called the Coal Age.
15. Some glaciers grew to be more than a mile high.

Think about it

Pretend you are in a small airplane flying low over the state of Illinois. Look down and tell what you see. What is the land like? What is the weather like? How are the waterways being used?

Find out

How is coal used today? Look in an encyclopedia or a library book about coal. Make drawings or cut pictures from magazines of products we get from coal. Make a display of your pictures.

In your neighborhood

As snow or ice melt around your school or home, watch for ways the water changes the soil nearby. If melting snow is not available, make a small pile of dirt or sand and place ice cubes on top of the pile. As the cubes melt, watch for ways the pile is changed by the running water.

Plan a garden for your yard. What plants would you like to grow? Make a list. Find out which of these plants would grow well in your area. Which ones could be started in your garden earliest? Get information from seed packets or from people who raise gardens. With permission, try growing some of the plants on your list.

CHAPTER 2

The People of Illinois

Young Illinoisans.

ILLINOIS DEPARTMENT OF COMMERCE AND COMMUNITY AFFAIRS

15

This picture shows early people in Illinois hollowing out tree trunks to build canoes.

People in Illinois come from many different ethnic backgrounds.

Our state's earliest people gathered their food from the land. This picture is taken from an exhibit at the Illinois State Museum.

LESSON 1

First People

People have lived in Illinois for more than 10,000 years. The people who came here about 8000 B.C. were looking for food. They must have been pleased. The rich soil left behind by the Ice Age glaciers made Illinois a good home. Plants and animals grew very well. The first people hunted the animals and gathered food from wild plants. Then they learned to store enough food in summer and fall so they did not have to move to find food in winter.

The people who lived here long ago did not know how to write. They did leave behind clues which *archeologists* are using to learn their story.

Archeologists have learned that two periods of time were very important in our state's past. They are the Hopewell and Mississippian periods. During these times, people in Illinois made important changes in the way they lived.

The Hopewell Period

The Hopewell Period began about 1000 B.C. It lasted until A.D. 500. Unlike others before them, these people had enough food to stay all year in one place. Most of their food came from wild plants and animals, but they also planted a few crops.

Living in one place made the Hopewell people different from those who had to move from place to place to find food. For one thing, the Hopewell took special care in the way they buried their dead. They formed large hills over the graves of their loved ones. Each hill contained many graves.

The Hopewell people wanted things they could not get where they lived. They began to trade with people far away. They got new supplies to make tools, weapons, and jewelry. Archeologists have found shells from the

This painting shows one kind of mound from the Mississippian Period.

Gulf of Mexico that they used for jewelry. They found stones of mica and copper. Mica is found near the Appalachian Mountains. The copper probably came from the land around Lake Superior. How do you think the people traveled in order to exchange these things?

Hopewell people were probably the first to use money in Illinois. They chipped pieces of flint into round, flat shapes. This money made trade easier.

The Mississippian Period

Another important time was the Mississippian Period. It lasted from about 900 to 1500. The people of this time are often called Mound Builders. Like the Hopewell people, they built huge mounds or hills. The shape of each hill meant something. There were cones, pyramids, and animals. Sometimes the hills were built in the shape of birds, snakes, lizards, or even people. Many of the hills covered graves. Often, religious buildings were built on top of the hills. Other mounds were used as forts. Some

INDIAN MOUNDS

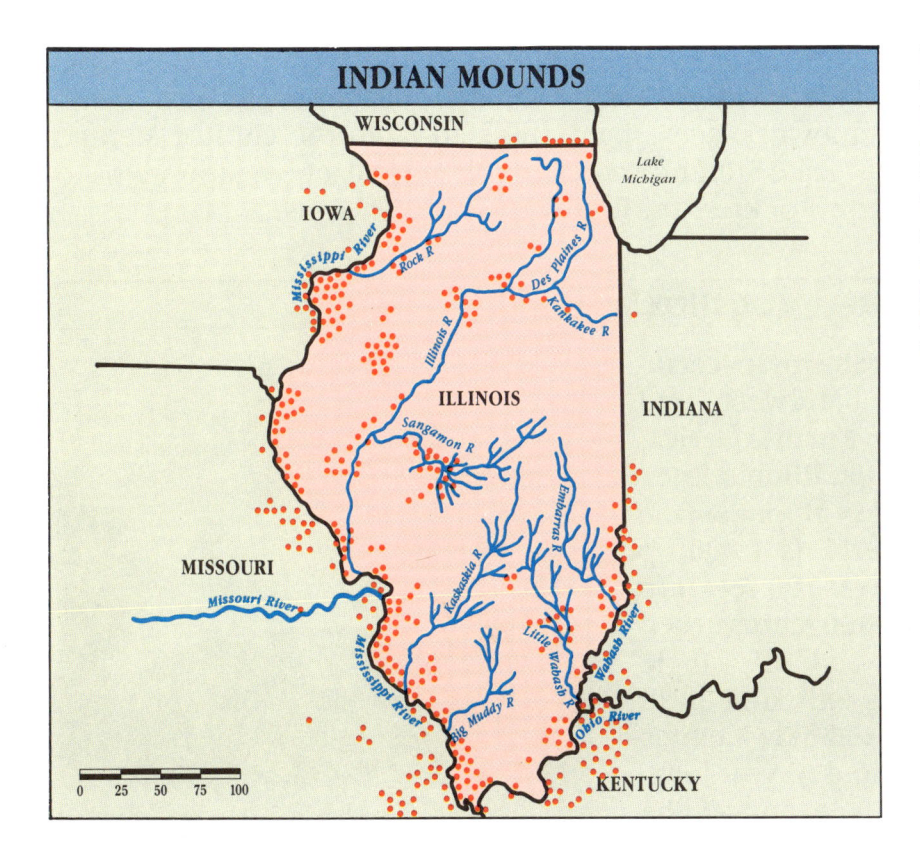

This map shows where Indians before 1600 built mounds in Illinois. Study the map. What general statement can you write about early Indians and the location of their villages?

of the mounds were so large they looked like natural hills. However, we know by their shapes that these hills were formed by people.

The number of people in Illinois grew during the Mississippian Period. The people still hunted and fished. They gathered wild rice and other wild foods. But for the first time, they grew most of their food. These were Illinois' first real farmers. Mississippian farmers grew squash, beans, and corn. Corn became their most important crop.

Some of the Mississippian people lived in large towns. Cahokia, the largest town, covered about five square miles. Other people lived in villages and on small farms. These farms and villages were spread over hundreds of miles around the larger towns.

As in the Hopewell Period, the Mississippian people traded widely. They used materials brought from many faraway places. They traveled from the Gulf of Mexico to Lake Superior and from the Appalachian Mountains to the Rockies, trading with other Indians.

CAHOKIA MOUNDS

The largest prehistoric earthworks in the Midwest, and possibly all of North America, are west of Collinsville, Illinois. They are known as Cahokia Mounds. One mound, Monk's Mound, is 1,000 by 720 feet in size. It rises 100 feet into the air. More than 1,000 men worked for five years to build this single earthwork. And it is only one of 80 mounds in the area. Cahokia Mounds State Park can be visited all year long. Special tours are given during the summer months.

Monk's Mound, near Cahokia, is the largest earthwork built by prehistoric Indians in North America.

DOING YOUR OWN DIGGING

At Kampsville, not far from Cahokia, Northwestern University is studying prehistoric Indians. What's unusual about that? At Kampsville, you can be the archeologist. That's right! Students can go to Kampsville and dig. They work with archeologists at the site of a prehistoric Indian village. If you're interested, contact the Center for American Archeology in Evanston, Illinois.

Students search for evidence of prehistoric Indians at the Koster Site near Kampsville.

LESSON 2

Woodland Indians

We do not know what became of the Mississippian people. Sickness, war, or *drought* may have caused the end of their way of life. One way or another, the Mound Builders disappeared from our land.

By 1600, Indians from the Eastern Woodlands took the place of the Mound Builders. The map on page 22 shows where these tribes lived. Being Woodland Indians meant the people made their homes in the forests and prairies. They hunted, fished, and farmed for their living.

Northern Indians

In the north, they depended more on wild foods than on farming. These tribes moved often. They went far to hunt buffalo and deer, to trade, and to make war.

In summer, northern Indians lived in large groups near rivers or lakes. The men fished and the women grew small gardens. Near the end of summer the women gathered their yearly harvest of wild rice and a few vegetables. Soon afterward, the families would prepare to move.

Model shows a Kickapoo Indian making a gun. Kickapoos lived in central Illinois from the late 1600s until 1834. By then the U.S. government had moved the last of them to lands in Missouri.

Each family would take apart their *wigwam* and roll up its birchbark cover.

During winter, each family would live alone or with one or two other families. They would move from place to place, hunting the herds of buffalo or deer. They walked or went by birchbark canoe. The women would carry along the rolls of bark to rebuild their homes in each new place. The families always stayed within their own tribe's hunting grounds.

Each Indian tribe moved from time to time. This map shows approximately where they were centered.

HISTORIC INDIAN TRIBES

The Kickapoos raised gardens, as did other southern tribes. They learned to grow watermelon, a native African plant.

Southern Indians

Further south, farming was more important. Most Indians in central and southern Illinois lived in year-round villages along the rivers. Their villages were made up of long, bark-covered lodges. A village might be a mile long, with more than a hundred lodges. Some larger villages had as many as 400 to 500 lodges. Like a row of apartments, each lodge was the home of several families. Inside, the people slept on beds built like shelves along the walls.

Outside the villages were fields. There the women grew large gardens of corn, beans, squash, and pumpkins. The men fished in nearby rivers and streams. In fall, the Indians sliced and dried squash and pumpkins. Some corn was dried, ground into meal, and stored in pits. Later, when there was more time, this corn would be ground into a meal called *hominy*. The hominy, dried pumpkin, and squash made up much of their winter food.

Fall was also a time to hunt. The men would go on long deer and buffalo hunts. As in the north, Indians hunting outside their tribe's own hunting grounds faced danger from other Indians.

Illini Alliance

The Kaskaskia, Michegamea, Peoria, Moingwena, Cahokia, and Tamaroa Indians formed an *alliance*. This group called itself Illini, which means "the men." From this group came the name of our state. The Illini tribes agreed to share their hunting grounds, to follow certain rules, and to help protect one another.

The Illini worked hard to protect members of their group. The wonderful hunting grounds of Illinois were like a magnet to outside Indian groups. Time after time, the Illini fought bravely to hold onto their land. Year after year, the powerful Illini were able to keep other tribes away.

However, word of the rich hunting grounds in Illinois spread all the way to New York. In the 1600s the Iroquois Indians came more than 500 miles to make war. They killed about 1,200 Illini. The Illini split in different directions and became weaker and smaller. Although the Iroquois did not stay here, they brought an end to our state's most powerful Indian alliance.

STARVED ROCK

Along the Illinois River between Ottawa and La Salle is Starved Rock State Park. Inside the park is a high, flat rock called Starved Rock. The way Starved Rock got its name is an interesting story.

In 1769, after the Illini alliance of Indians had lost much of its power, a small group of Illini Indians were surrounded while on top of the rock. They knew they could defend themselves easily from the enemy tribe below. The rock stood high above the river and could only be reached from one side. On the other three sides, there was a drop of more than 150 feet to the river below. To get water, they used long vines to lower their water vessels to the Illinois River.

Their plan did not work. Some of their enemies hid near the base of the rock. They cut the vines each time the Illini tried to get water from the river. One by one the Illini died from lack of water and food. They chose to starve rather than give themselves up to their enemies.

EUROPEAN LAND CLAIMS

Legend:
- English Claim
- French Claim
- Spanish Claim
- Unexplored

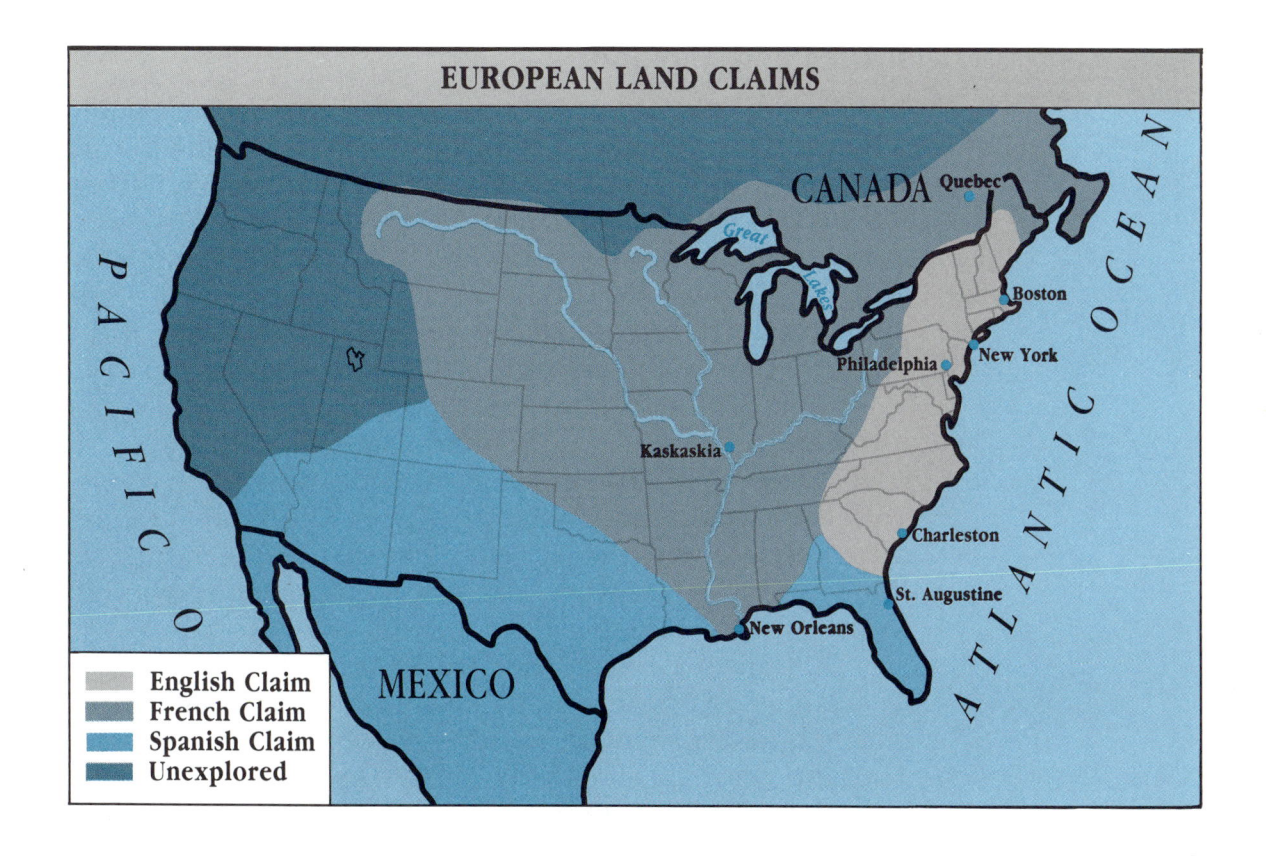

LESSON 3

Illinois: Home for Many People

The rich farmland and hunting grounds attracted people other than Indians. At first, they trickled in. Then they came in wave after wave. They came from the eastern United States and all over the world.

After Columbus visited North America in 1492, several European countries sent people to settle in this land. By 1673 much of our *continent* was claimed by three countries. Look at the map above. England, France, and Spain each held huge parts of North America. Europeans lived on very little of this land. Some had not even been explored. Except along the coasts, most of North America was *inhabited* by Indians.

Jolliet and Marquette

Illinois was part of the French claim. In 1673 the French governor of Canada sent Louis Jolliet (jahl-ee-ET), an expert mapmaker, to find out where the Mississippi River led. Father Jacques Marquette (mar-KET), a priest, was asked to go along. He would be able to help Jolliet talk with the Indians. He had lived in Canada for seven years and had learned to speak many Indian languages. Marquette would also teach the Indians about Christianity.

Jolliet and Marquette paddled across Lake Michigan into Green Bay in two birchbark canoes. With the help of five French boatmen, they followed Wisconsin rivers until they found the Mississippi River. Then they floated down the Mississippi River past the southern tip of Illinois. When they were sure that the Mississippi flowed to the Gulf of Mexico, they turned back.

On their way back, they paddled up the Illinois and DesPlaines rivers through the center of Illinois. They returned to Canada with exciting news. The soil was rich. The land was flat. Trees did not have to be cleared before houses could be built.

Jolliet and Marquette had visited Indian villages near today's cities of Peoria and Ottawa. Father Marquette promised the Indians at Kaskaskia village that he would return to teach them about Christianity. In 1675 he did so, and began the first *mission* in Illinois near Kaskaskia.

More French follow

After Marquette and Jolliet's trip, other French people came to Illinois. Some were trappers who searched the rivers of Illinois for furs to be sold in Europe. Others were priests, merchants, and farmers who set up more missions, trading posts, and small villages. The first two permanent European settlements were set up by the French at Cahokia in 1699 and Kaskaskia in 1703. Other small villages, such as Prairie du Rocher, grew up around French forts.

Marquette and Jolliet float down the Mississippi River with their Indian guides.

The French changed the way Indians lived. They no longer hunted animals only for their own food and clothes. Now they also hunted for furs to trade at the French trading posts.

Blacks—slave and free

In 1720 the first black people came to Illinois. They were brought as slaves by a Frenchman. By 1752 there were about 450 black people in Illinois working as servants, craftsmen, and farmers.

France lost Illinois to England in 1763. Life changed little under English rule. Only a handful of people came from England or the English colonies in North America to live in Illinois.

About the time England took over, a black Frenchman came to Illinois from New Orleans, Louisiana. He was Jean Baptiste DuSable. DuSable was a free man, but he was afraid that slave owners would think he was a runaway slave. He did not want to be captured and made a slave. He moved to Illinois and lived with the Illini Indians. Later, he moved to northern Illinois and lived among the Potawatomi. DuSable married a Potawatomi Indian, Kittihawa, and became a member of her tribe.

About 1779 DuSable and his wife moved to the southern tip of Lake Michigan. There they set up a trading post. They built a house, barn, two stables, workshop, smokehouse, poultry house, and mill. French, Indian, and English traders all came to DuSable's post to do business. Jean Baptiste DuSable's settlement was the beginning of the city of Chicago.

Illinois—a new beginning

In 1818 Illinois became the twenty-first state to join the United States. People began to move here in large numbers. Some came from other parts of the United States while many, called *immigrants,* came here from other countries. Thousands of immigrants, like those who came from Ireland, left their homelands to escape *famine* and hard times. Many found work in mills and mines or in large towns as laborers.

In the 1840s and 1850s, several groups set up separate communities for their people. Three of these in Illinois are well known. First was the village of Bourbonnais. Bourbonnais was started near where Kankakee is today. It became the home of a group of Catholic French-Canadians who were unhappy with their lives in Canada.

Jean Baptiste DuSable.

Visitors at Bishop Hill.

Bishop Hill was to be an ideal home for followers of Eric Janson. The Jansonists were from Sweden. They did not agree with the Lutheran church. But it was the only church allowed in Sweden at that time. This group settled Bishop Hill, which is between Galesburg and Moline. There they could live and worship in their own way.

THE CLOCK WITH ONE HAND

There's a strange legend about Bishop Hill. The steeple clock has only one hand—the hour hand. The legend says that the Swedish immigrants didn't need the minute hand. They worked so hard they only needed the hour hand to tell time. They didn't worry about minutes.

Today Bishop Hill is much like it was in 1850. When you visit the town, you can watch demonstrations of spinning, broommaking, and wood carving. If you come in September during *Jordbruksdagarna,* you can enjoy hand-pressed cider and eat delicious Swedish foods. Other special days at Bishop Hill are *Jul Marknad* (Christmas Market) and *Lucia Nights*. Costumed girls wearing crowns of candles serve coffee and cookies at this festival of lights in December.

Another group, called Mormons, also came to Illinois to find religious freedom. They did not come from another country, but moved from New York to Ohio and then Missouri.

Thousands of Mormons crossed the Mississippi River and bought land in Illinois. They built the town of Nauvoo. Nauvoo grew to have more people than any other town in Illinois, until the Mormons left for Utah in 1846.

NAUVOO

Joseph Smith founded the Mormon church. In Missouri, Smith and his church had been threatened and attacked. They left Missouri for safety. They started the town of Nauvoo, Illinois, so they could worship in their own way.

Fifteen thousand Mormons lived in Nauvoo. It was the largest city in Illinois. Other Illinoisans became worried. Many feared that the Mormons, voting as a group, could control the state government. Fear of the church's power led to stories of laws being broken by the Mormons. The stories turned to charges against Smith, and he was arrested twice.

In 1844 Joseph Smith and his brother Hyrum were put into the Carthage jail. A mob of people broke into the jail. Guards did little to stop them. The two brothers were killed. After their deaths, many Mormons left Illinois for a land called Utah.

Joseph Smith is shot to death by a mob at the Carthage jail while soldiers sent to protect him look on.

People from Germany came to Illinois after their crops failed in their home country. Many were able to get land to farm. Others got jobs in the larger towns. Because so many Germans came, a law was passed to allow people to teach the German language in schools.

Slaves seek freedom

During the early 1800s, free blacks and runaway slaves came to Illinois. Many just passed through our state on their way to freedom in Canada. They were helped on their way by the people of Illinois. Some blacks stayed in Illinois. They took their chances that people in this *free state* would not turn them in as runaway slaves.

The question of slavery in the United States was settled by the Civil War in 1865. All states would be free states and ex-slaves were made citizens.

More immigrants arrive

From 1870 to 1920, immigrants poured into the United States. Millions came from around the world. At first, most of them came from England, Ireland, Germany and Sweden. They came because work was hard to find at home and Illinois promised them a new start in life. Soon new groups of immigrants joined them. Poles, Austrians, Bohemians, Russians, Jews, Italians, Greeks, and Romanians came from Europe. Chinese and Japanese came from Asia. Mexicans also came hoping to find work. Thousands came to Illinois. They left hard times in their own countries. All hoped to find a better life here. Some farmed as they had done before. But many went to work in the mills and factories. They worked in mines and steel mills, in farm machinery factories, and in meat-packing plants. Some worked on trolley lines. New people helped build canals, skyscrapers, roads, and thousands of miles of railroads.

Illinois and its cities grew quickly with the help of these new Americans. Then in 1921, the United States government passed a law to cut down the number of people who could come into this country. By that time, Illinois had a rich mix of different *ethnic groups.* More than half of our state's four million people had been born somewhere besides Illinois.

Immigrants and Americans from other states still come to Illinois today. Some come from Europe and Asia, but not as many as before 1921. Some come from Mexico and other Spanish-language countries. Since 1970 another group of newcomers have come to Illinois to start a new life. These are Vietnamese and Laotian people who left their homes to escape the fighting and destruction of war.

Illinois is a *melting pot.* People from all over the world are changed into Americans and Illinoisans while living and working in Illinois. They learn new laws and new things that are expected of them. They become like other citizens of Illinois. They also add new ingredients to the melting pot. Their new ways of doing things help make Illinois an interesting and exciting place to live.

Immigrants at the Barrett Company took an English class after working all day.

Hull House was an organization that helped immigrants. This dance in 1916 was one of many activities Hull House sponsored.

34

DO YOU REMEMBER?

Words worth remembering

Match the word from the chapter with its meaning.

1. famine
2. alliance
3. drought
4. ethnic group
5. immigrant

A. a very dry time when plants don't grow
B. a person who moves into a country to live
C. people who agree to work together for a common goal
D. an extreme lack of food
E. people of similar race, religion, or history

Ideas to remember

Fill in the blank with the word from the WORD BANK that correctly completes the sentence.

6. _____ learn what life was like long ago by studying things buried in the ground.
7. Chipped pieces of flint were the first money used by the _____ people.
8. The Mississippians are also called _____ because of the hills they formed into unusual shapes.
9. The Woodland Indians made their living by farming and _____ .
10. The first farmers in Illinois were the _____ .
11. _____ was a mapmaker who explored for France.
12. The _____ defeated the Illini alliance.
13. _____ started a trading post on the site of Chicago.
14. Illinois is called a _____ because so many ethnic groups live here.
15. Indians hunted animals to _____ with the French.

Word bank

Jolliet

melting pot

archeologists

Mississippians

Mound Builders

Iroquois

hunting

trade

Hopewell

DuSable

Think about it

Make your own personal time line. Record 10 important events in your life by placing them in the right spot on your time line.

Find out

Find out more about a subject listed below and make a model or diorama.

    How Starved Rock got its name

    DuSable's trading post

    Map of the journey of Marquette and Jolliet

    An Indian wigwam

    An Indian lodge

    An Illinois mission

In your neighborhood

Take a survey of your block. Interview only people you already know. Find out where their ancestors came from. Put your data on a bar graph. Use a different bar for each country.

CHAPTER

3

The Early Years

View from the Illinois–Michigan Canal.

View of Chicago in 1833. What does this sketch tell you about the city's history?

French trappers made friends with Illinois Indians in order to get animal furs.

LESSON 1

Under Three Flags

You have learned that the French were the first Europeans to live in Illinois. France had several reasons for wanting to settle here. First, French fur traders in Canada wanted to expand their business south of the Great Lakes. From the Indians, the French got furs that they sold for a lot of money in Europe. The Indians got beads, cloth, knives, and hatchets. These items cost very little back in France. But they saved the Indians a lot of time and work. So the fur trade was good for both the French and Indians.

France's second reason was religion. Like Father Marquette, other missionaries wanted to teach Christianity to the many Indians in Illinois.

The French wanted Illinois for another reason, too. They dreamed of a huge *empire* in North America. To have an empire, France knew it must stop England from becoming too powerful. So France planned to control the middle of North America. Illinois was to be a part of that empire.

LaSalle and Tonti

Robert Cavalier de LaSalle (kav-uhl-YAY duh-luh-SAL) was asked to settle Illinois for France. Excited by news of Marquette and Jolliet's trip, LaSalle made plans to develop the area. First he would start a fur trading company so the Indians would only trade with France. Then he would build a chain of forts from the St. Lawrence River to the *mouth* of the Mississippi River. The king of France was pleased. He gave LaSalle land in Canada and put him in charge of the fur trade south of the Great Lakes.

In fall of 1679, LaSalle and an Italian friend, Henri de Tonti (hen-REE day tohn-TEE), led a group of men into Illinois. Near Utica, Illini Indians prepared a feast for LaSalle. He and his men spent the night as the Indians' guests. Then they went on. They built Fort Crevecoeur (KREV-kur) near Peoria. Putting Tonti in charge of Fort Crevecoeur, LaSalle went back to Canada for supplies.

LaSalle claimed for France all the land touched by the Mississippi River.

Tonti's trouble

While LaSalle was gone, Tonti ran into trouble. Many of the men began to worry that LaSalle could not pay them. They angrily destroyed the fort. Taking weapons and ammunition, they left Tonti with no fort and only five men.

That was only the beginning of Tonti's troubles. The Iroquois came all the way from New York to make war on the Illini Indians. When the Iroquois attacked, Tonti was mistaken for an Illini warrior. Before he could escape, Tonti was stabbed by an Iroquois brave.

In 1682 LaSalle and Tonti returned to Illinois. They only stayed for a short time. LaSalle wanted to be the first to travel down the Mississippi River to the Gulf of Mexico. There he claimed the land on both sides of the Mississippi for his king, Louis. LaSalle called the land Louisiana.

Back the travelers came to Illinois. On top of Starved Rock, LaSalle and his men built Fort St. Louis. Thousands of Illini Indians built their homes in sight of LaSalle's fort for protection against the Iroquois.

LaSalle's new plan

LaSalle returned to France. He had a new plan. He promised the king he would build a *colony* at the mouth of the Mississippi River. It would stop the country of Spain from entering Louisiana.

The king gave LaSalle four ships. LaSalle left France with 200 people. They sailed into the Gulf of Mexico, but missed the mouth of the Mississippi. They landed instead on the coast of Texas. The people were angry. Some went back to France. Others shot and killed LaSalle when he could not lead them to the mouth of the river.

Tonti took over LaSalle's work in Illinois. He built a larger Fort St. Louis near Lake Peoria. But he could not get many French people to make their homes in Illinois. It wasn't until 1720, when Fort de Chartres (duh-SHAR-truh) was built, that the French villages grew.

French life in early Illinois is demonstrated each year at the Fort de Chartres Rendezvous.

Fort de Chartres was built near Kaskaskia. The stone fort protected farmers, trappers, traders and missionaries from unfriendly Indians. It helped make trade safe between Illinois and the new French town of New Orleans, at the mouth of the Mississippi. Still, there were never more than about 2,000 French people in Illinois.

Life in French villages

French villages in Illinois were made up of small houses along narrow streets or paths. The houses were built close together for safety. At the center of most villages was a church. Often the priest served as the school teacher for the village.

French houses

There were two kinds of houses. The *gentry* built houses of stone. The common people, called *habitants,* built homes with wooden frames and cross strips. Straw mixed with clay filled the spaces between cross strips. All the houses had steep roofs covered with straw or thin pieces of wood. Most had a single door, two or three windows,

This drawing of a French house in Kaskaskia appeared in a French magazine in 1826. Would this home be for the gentry or habitants?

COURTESY OF THE ILLINOIS STATE HISTORICAL LIBRARY

and a clay or log floor. A wide porch sometimes ran all the way around the house. Finally, the house was *whitewashed* many times, inside and out.

Inside, a house was divided into two rooms. In one room was a fireplace for heating and cooking. The other was a bedroom. A ladder led to the attic, where the children slept on feather beds or straw.

Outside the village, each family had a long, narrow strip of land reaching to the river bank. This allowed every family access to the river for water and transportation. Each village also had a large pasture where cattle and horses grazed.

French food

The whole family helped with the farming. The French had learned from the Indians to grow corn, beans, squash, pumpkins, and melons. They ate these foods and fed them to their animals. The French ate some meat, mostly pork or dried beef. They added to their meat supply by hunting and fishing. Butter was a special treat. It was made by beating cream with a spoon or shaking it in a bottle.

Because the land of Illinois was so good for farming, French families had crops to sell. Wheat, oats, and tobacco grew well in the rich soil. Along with bacon, buffalo hides, and furs, these crops were sent to New Orleans. There they were sold. Sugar, rice, furniture, tools, and clothing were brought back to the villages.

Work in the French towns

Everyone was busy when there was planting or harvesting to do. Between busy seasons, men trapped animals for the fur companies. They went on hunting trips or traded with the Indians. Some worked on boats going up and down the Mississippi River.

At these times, the women worked on clothing. They sewed red and blue cotton dresses for themselves and their daughters. They made blue *homespun* shirts and *pantaloons* for the men and boys. They made deerskin moccasins for the whole family.

The French at play

The villagers visited each other on Sundays after church. Everyone, young and old, sang folk songs, danced, and played cards. They had many parties, especially on holidays. The yearly arrival of goods from France was as exciting as any holiday. The whole village turned out when the boat came into sight.

"Papa! Mama!" the children would shout. "Hurry! Hurry! It's coming!" The whole family would rush to the dock. It would be a full year before they would again see so many tools, furniture, and fabrics.

A celebration in a French village near Kaskaskia.

> **LEAD MINES**
>
> When Chicago was just a trading post, over 10,000 men were mining lead near Galena. Galena is the name for lead sulphide ore. When this ore is heated, lead is produced. Lead was used to make water pipes and tools. Bullets were also made from lead. Today lead is used in batteries, gasoline and X-ray equipment.

They spent their money carefully. First came tools, then plenty of red and blue cotton for the year's clothes. Those with more money could buy coffee and maybe some silk or satin and lace for party dresses. Only the gentry had enough money to buy a piece of fine carved furniture.

Most of the time, the French people in Illinois did not need to be protected from the Indians. The Illini and most other tribes generally got along well with the French. Together they fished, hunted, trapped, and explored. Because of the missionaries, some Indians went to French churches. Many French fur traders married Indian women.

Slavery

In 1720 Philippe Renault (Fil-EEP Ren-OH) brought slaves to Illinois. Renault planned to start mines where there might be gold or other valuable minerals.

Renault stopped in the West Indies and bought some black slaves. He planned to use slaves for the hardest work in his mines. He would use other slaves to farm his land and grow food for the miners.

Renault, his slaves, and other miners started to mine lead at the mouth of the Galena River. The demand for lead was great. Renault was allowed to buy more slaves. In 1724 he was sent 50 black people. In return he promised to send 15,000 pounds of lead to New Orleans.

Before Renault returned to France, he sold his slaves

to French villagers. For the next 100 years, some Illinoisans kept black people as slaves. The number of slaves grew, but never reached more than about 500 to 600.

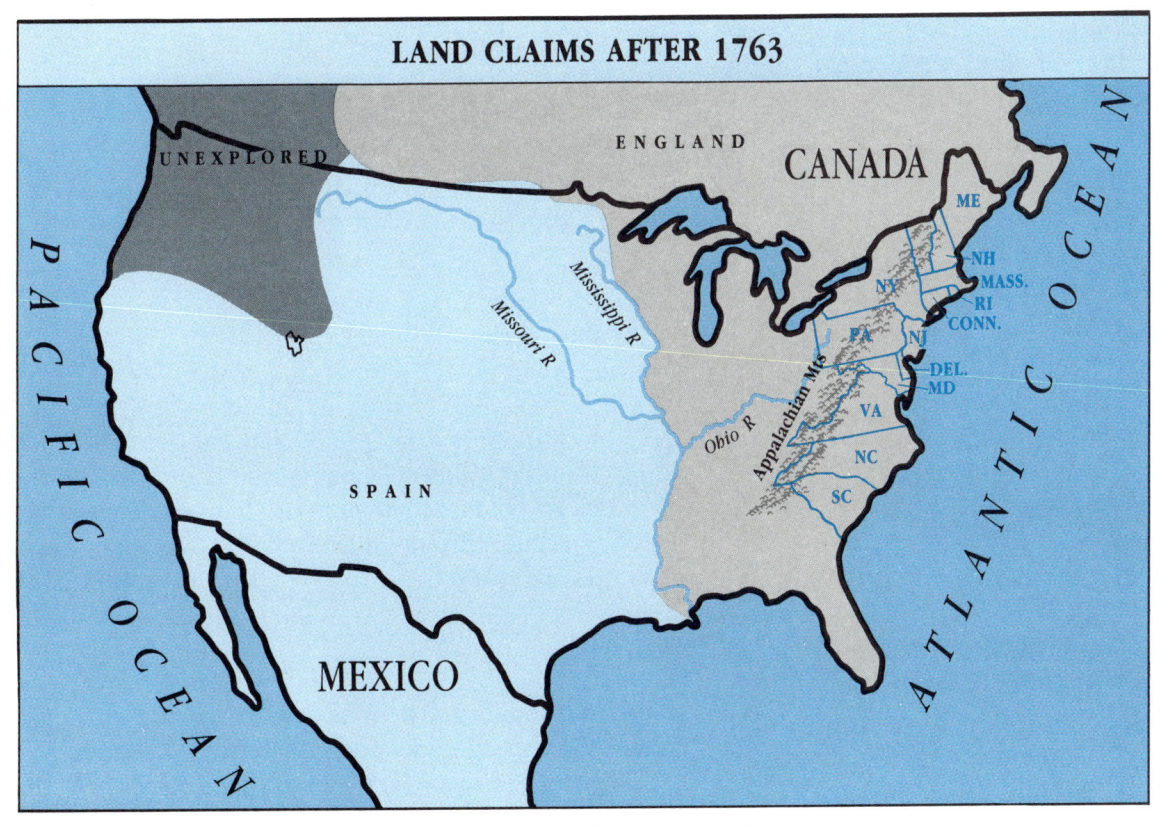

LAND CLAIMS AFTER 1763

Most people lived in the English colonies in 1763. Few people settled as far west as Illinois.

LESSON 2

Illinois Changes Hands

French and Indian War

For years France and England fought each other in different places around the world. In North America, the fighting was called the French and Indian War. Both sides were helped by Indians. Algonquin Indians fought on the side of the French. Iroquois Indians helped the English. After nine years, the English won. France agreed that all land between the Appalachian Mountains and Mississippi River now belonged to England. England was also given Canada. Illinois was now in English hands.

Many French people were not willing to live under English rule. Some left North America and went back to France. Many moved west of the Mississippi River or south to New Orleans. Other French people stayed, not knowing what would happen to them.

Soon after the war ended, King George of England signed a special law. He would not let English settlers into the lands just won from the French. England was afraid of trouble with Indians. Many were still friends of the French. English soldiers took over the French forts. But before the Indian problem could be solved, England was at war again. This time they were fighting against their own colonies.

The American Revolution

In 1776 England's thirteen colonies on the Atlantic coast of North America *declared* their *independence*. They named themselves the United States of America. Of course, just saying they were free did not bring freedom. The Americans had to fight a war to gain freedom from English rule.

Most of the fighting took place in the thirteen colonies. However, battles were also fought west of the

Appalachian Mountains. George Rogers Clark made sure Illinois would not stay in English hands.

Clark had moved to Kentucky from Virginia. He was worried about the English in the forts at Kaskaskia in Illinois and at Vincennes in Indiana. They could attack Americans in Kentucky at any time. Clark asked for help. The governor of Virginia told Clark to raise an army.

Clark could get only 175 Kentuckians to go with him. The tiny army set out for the English forts. They floated down the Ohio River. About 120 miles from Kaskaskia, they left their boats and went by foot. Six days later, they could see the fort. They hid until dark. That night they surprised the English soldiers and took the fort without firing a shot.

A long march

After the victory Clark was still worried. Surely the English would attack him at Kaskaskia in the spring. Many of his soldiers had signed up for only a few months. Most of them were gone. His small army would never be able to hold off an English attack. He would have to attack first. His success would depend on surprise. No one would expect him to march during the winter.

Clark had less than 200 men. Almost half of them were French habitants who had never been soldiers. In early February 1779, the little army set out on foot toward Vincennes. The trip took almost three weeks. They waded through mud and water sometimes a foot or two deep, sometimes up to their necks. They had to be careful not to be seen by unfriendly Indians. That meant camping with no fires to dry and warm them. Clark had to work day and night to keep up the men's spirits. With a week of marching left, they ran out of food. They went five days with only one deer to eat.

On the evening of 24 February, the weary army reached Vincennes. They attacked the fort! The British could not believe they had been attacked by such a small

CLARK'S ROUTE

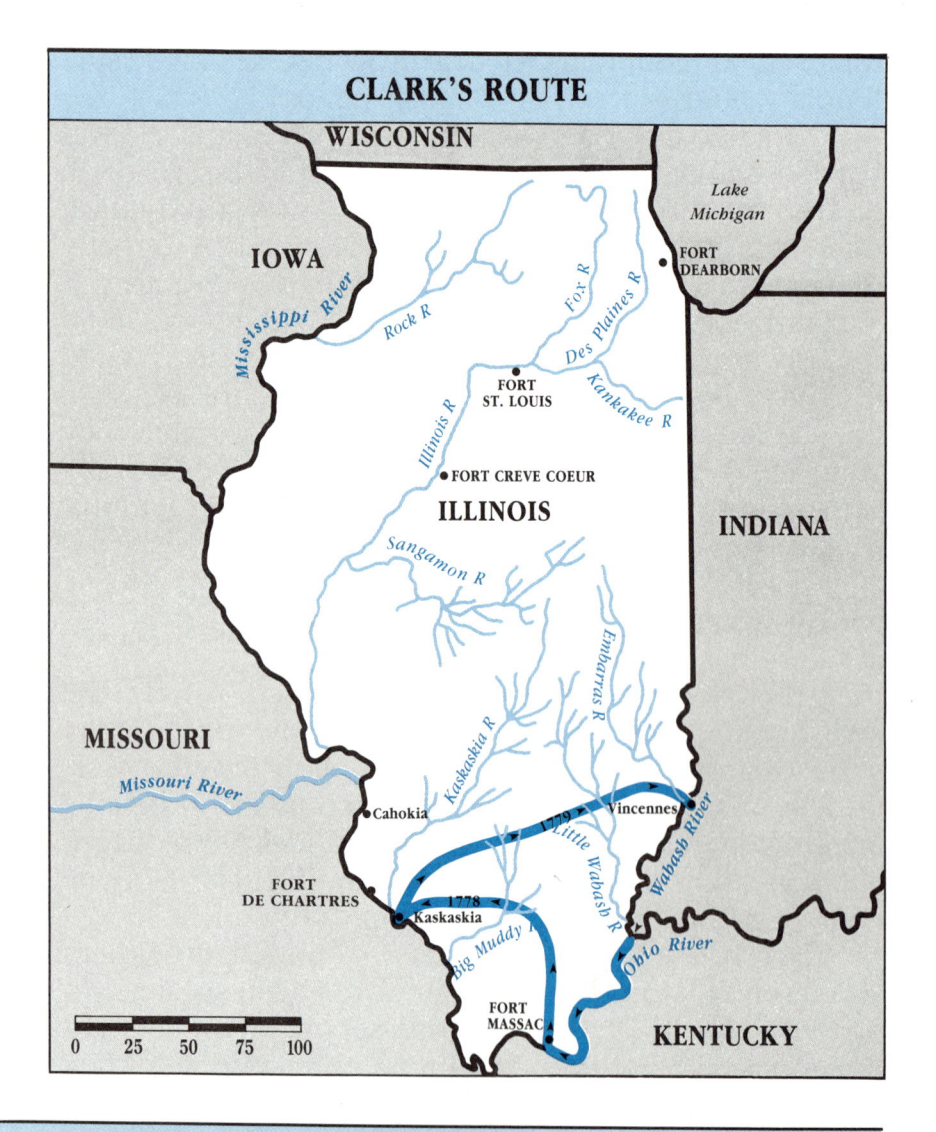

DECLARATION OF INDEPENDENCE

The Declaration of Independence explained why the colonies wanted to be free from England. Thomas Jefferson did most of the writing. He explained that people have rights which no one can take away—not even a king. These are life, liberty, and the chance to live a happy life. And since governments get their power from the people, the people can change the government if necessary. On 4 July 1776, the colonial government accepted Jefferson's work.

George Rogers Clark and his men crossing the Wabash River just before their attack on the French at Vincennes, Indiana.

army. They turned over the fort to Clark the next afternoon.

The Revolutionary War lasted for seven years. Americans won their independence. The country stretched from the Atlantic Ocean to the Mississippi River. Illinois was a part of the new United States of America.

A United States territory

The new United States had thirteen states and plenty of land. In 1785 the United States set up a plan to divide and sell its western lands.

Pioneers had already begun moving westward from the Atlantic Ocean to settle on new land. Some of the men who had fought with George Rogers Clark stayed in Illinois. Others returned to their homes in Kentucky. Their glowing reports of the beautiful, rich land in southern Illinois attracted other Americans. They came in great covered wagons or on huge *flatboats*. They followed easy lines of travel along the Ohio, Wabash, Illinois, and Mississippi rivers. Americans came from Kentucky, Virginia, and Pennsylvania. Southern Illinois began filling up.

Flatboats brought thousands of families to Illinois.

New families who came to Illinois found rich farm land and plenty of animals to hunt. But they did not find a government. The United States was so new it had not yet created a plan for the land near the Mississippi River. In 1787 a plan was made setting up the Northwest Territory. The people in the territory would have to follow the laws of the United States. They could meet together to make rules to solve their special problems. When 60,000 people lived in a part of the territory, it could ask to become a state.

Fort Dearborn is built

In northern Illinois, Jean Baptiste du DuSable had been forced to leave his trading post during the Revolutionary War. After the war, he returned and stayed until 1800. A few Americans settled near DuSable's trading post next to the Chicago River and Lake Michigan. Fear of Indian attack, however, kept the number of people in the area small.

In 1803, three years after DuSable left his trading post, the United States built Fort Dearborn where the Chicago River enters Lake Michigan. A trader named John Kinzie moved his family into DuSable's cabin. They took over the trading post. Very slowly other pioneers began moving into the area.

NORTHWEST TERRITORY

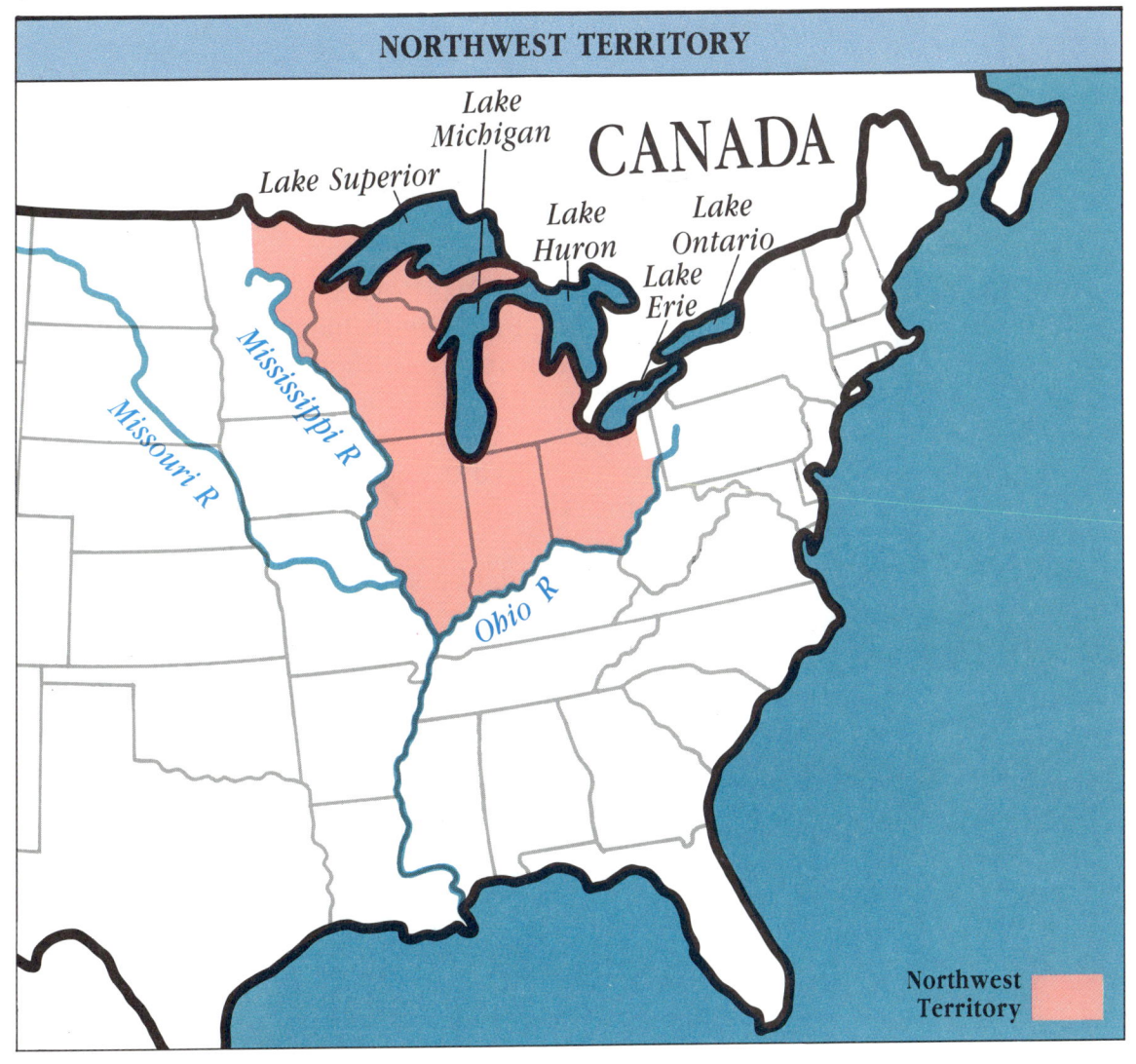

Before the Revolutionary War, the Northwest Territory had been Indian land. Now Americans poured in, taking away more and more land. The Indians were upset. Most of them had helped the French, English, or Americans in their wars with one another. Yet Indians were not invited to the meetings to decide who should own the land. Angry Indians attacked American settlements. Sometimes they killed settlers. Often they stole horses, tore down fences, and destroyed crops.

War of 1812

The English still hoped to end the Americans' dream of being independent. Another war between the United States and England began. Angry Indians fought along with the English. They wanted to drive the Americans out of their land. In all of Illinois, the tiny settlement at Fort Dearborn suffered most.

The soldiers at Fort Dearborn were ordered to go to Fort Wayne, Indiana. Friendly Indians warned them not to go. There were not many soldiers. They would have to travel with ten to fifteen families past many unfriendly tribes. John Kinzie and other settlers agreed. It would be too dangerous. They had enough food and guns to stay in the fort for months. But the commander said he must obey his orders.

On 15 August 1812, the soldiers and settlers started for Fort Wayne. Before they had gone two miles, they were attacked by Indians. A bloody battle followed. The Indians killed or captured everyone in the group. Then they burned the fort. This battle has become known as the Fort Dearborn Massacre.

The war ended in 1814. The English could not capture the land they once ruled over. Most of the fighting between settlers and Indians also ended.

The Fort Dearborn Massacre was painted by Frederick Glass in 1933.

NEW STATES—NEW NAMES

Thomas Jefferson had a plan for naming the states west of the Appalachian Mountains. He wanted to use Greek and Indian names. Under his plan, Chicago would be in the state of Assenisipia today. Springfield would be located in Illinoia. Carbondale would be in Polypotamia. Other states would be named Chersonesus, Metropotamia, Michigania, and Sylvania.

LESSON 3

Illinois Becomes A State

With the end of fighting, Americans rushed into Illinois. As the number of people grew, so did their interest in becoming a state.

In 1809 the Northwest Territory had been divided into two parts—Illinois and Indiana. The Indiana Territory had enough people in 1816 to become a state. Two years later a *census* showed that there were 40,259 people living in Illinois. That was enough people to become a state! The United States government admitted Illinois into the union as its 21st state in 1818.

Kaskaskia, one of Illinois' most important towns, was chosen as its *capital.* Here the *convention* met in 1818 to write the state's first *constitution.* Here Shadrach Bond became the first governor, and the first *legislators* took office.

Two years later, in 1820, the capital was moved to Vandalia. *Surveyors* were hired, and a brand new town was laid out. At its center, space was left to be used by the state government. By the end of the year, a *capitol* was built and the government moved to Vandalia. Vandalia remained the state capital until 1839, when it was moved to Springfield.

The Black Hawk War

After the War of 1812, few Indians stayed in Illinois. They

ILLINOIS' CAPITALS

CHICAGO—ILLINOIS OR WISCONSIN?

Can you imagine Illinois without Chicago? It could have happened. The plan to make Illinois a state showed its northern boundary near the southern tip of Lake Michigan. But Illinois had a wise delegate in Washington, D.C. Nathaniel Pope asked that Illinois' boundary be moved 40 miles north. If not for Pope, Chicago, Rockford, and other northern cities would be in Wisconsin.

lived where they could be by themselves. The Sauk and Fox tribes lived in the Rock Island area. Winnebago and Potawatomi remained around Prophetstown. By 1829 more land around Rock Island was being sold to white settlers. They wanted the Indians to leave. Some settlers even destroyed crops and burned the homes of Indians. President Andrew Jackson ordered the Sauk and Fox Indians to move west of the Mississippi River. Some of them protested, but the tribes moved to Iowa.

In the spring of 1832, the Sauk and Fox Indians needed food. Their corn crop of 1831 had failed. There had also been a bad hunting season. A group of Indians decided to come back to Illinois and plant corn with their Potawatomi and Winnebago friends. About 1,000 Indians gathered to cross the Mississippi. They were led by a 65-year-old Sauk Indian named Black Hawk. Black Hawk was not a chief, but his age and bravery were well respected.

The group included women and children. It was not a war party. But the braves were armed to protect their families. News of armed Indians nearby caused many Americans to panic. Soldiers were called out. Over 8,000 men were called to serve, including Abraham Lincoln. The Black Hawk War began. It lasted only three months, but close to 600 people lost their lives. About 500 of them were Indians.

The Indians had little chance against the soldiers and their better weapons. Black Hawk was captured. He, his followers, and the Winnebago and Potawatomi tribes were forced to give up their land in Illinois. All Indians had to move west of the Mississippi. Black Hawk and his people were put on a *reservation* in Iowa.

New attractions

In the ten years after the Black Hawk War, three things helped new settlers decide to live in Illinois. First, all Indian villages had been removed from Illinois. This brought an end to fighting among Indians and settlers in our state.

Black Hawk, a brave Sauk, led his tribe in search of more food.

The old capitol at Kaskaskia fell into the Mississippi River years after Vandalia became the seat of state government.

Second, transportation got better and easier. Steamboat travel, which started in 1811, improved. New routes opened. In 1825 the Erie Canal was built in New York. People could go by water from the Atlantic Ocean, up the Hudson River, to the Great Lakes. Once on the Great Lakes they could sail all the way to Chicago. Land travel also improved. Between 1825 and 1838, the government in Washington, D.C., extended the Cumberland Road from Ohio all the way to Vandalia, Illinois.

Third, new inventions made prairie farming easier. Plowing the tough sod had always been back-breaking work. Wooden plows could not cut through the thick roots of the tall prairie grass. Iron plows were not much better. The rich prairie soil stuck to them like glue. A farmer had to stop plowing often to scrape soil from the plow. Two Illinois men, John Deere and Harvey Henry May, found a solution. Both invented steel plows in 1837. May won the right to *patent* the steel plow, but Deere is generally remembered as its inventor.

John Deere was a *blacksmith* who made farm tools in Vermont. In 1836 he came to Grand Detour, Illinois. Deere saw the farmers' problem. He wondered if he could make a plow that would clean itself. He made a curved steel blade from a broken saw. Farmers came to watch Deere try out his new plow. Success! The soil slid right off the polished steel blade.

In 1847 Deere opened a factory in Moline, Illinois. His business grew quickly. Not only did his plow work well, Deere advertised his invention all over the United States. Soon Deere's factory was making 10,000 plows a year.

That same year, Cyrus Hall McCormick moved from Virginia to Chicago. He built a *reaper* factory. McCormick's reaper and the level Illinois prairie were made for each other. With John Deere's plow, Illinois farmers could plow large fields and plant large crops. With McCormick's machine, they could harvest as much grain as they could

HOW THE REAPER WORKS

A rider on a horse pulled a sled through the field of wheat. On the front of the sled were four boards which turned as the horse moved forward. Each board pushed wheat stems against a sharp blade. As the wheat was cut, a second worker raked the wheat into piles. The piles were tied and put on a wagon.

COURTESY CHICAGO HISTORICAL SOCIETY, DN, 59,411

plant. Wheat joined corn as a major crop. Illinois was on its way to becoming a leading agricultural state. By 1850 Illinois produced more wheat than any other northern state.

Chicago starts to grow

Farming was a major reason Chicago began to grow. In 1833 Chicago was a little town with only 350 people in about 150 houses. It covered less than half a square mile. Four years later, in 1837, Chicago became a city. At that time it had 4,000 people and an area of ten square miles. As Chicago grew, work began on a canal to connect Lake Michigan with the Illinois River. People and products, especially farm products, could be easily moved through the canal. Chicago's population grew as immigrants, many from Ireland, came to help dig the new canal.

Every year more people poured into Chicago. In 1847 McCormick's new reaper plant hired hundreds of workers. The next year, two new transportation lines to Chicago were finished. The Illinois and Michigan Canal linked Chicago with LaSalle and other cities in central Illinois. The Galena and Chicago Union Railroad began use of its first nine-mile stretch of track. Other railroads were already being built. Before long, the railroads would help make Chicago a business giant in the middle of the United States.

THE ILLINOIS-MICHIGAN CANAL

Horses pulled boats through the canal and its 17 locks. Each lock raised or lowered boats to the next level of the canal. Each boat was charged a toll to make the 30-hour trip between Chicago and LaSalle. The 60-foot-long boats were often crowded with passengers, their belongings, and their animals.

COURTESY OF THE ILLINOIS STATE HISTORICAL LIBRARY

Chicago was booming! The canal, factories, and railroads created thousands of jobs. More workers brought their families to Chicago. More houses, stores, streets, schools, and churches had to be built. By 1850 more than 30,000 people lived in Chicago!

Problems

Growth also brought problems to our state. In the 1800s slavery became a bigger and bigger problem. Our state constitution did not allow slavery. Yet Illinois was divided on the issue. People from all over had settled Illinois. Those from states that allowed slavery often agreed with the people "back home." People from free states wanted an end to slavery.

In 1837 a newspaper *editor* named Elijah Lovejoy moved from St. Louis, Missouri, to Alton, Illinois. He had been attacked twice for speaking out against slavery. But he was no safer in Illinois than he had been in Missouri. Twice mobs destroyed his printing press. They threatened to tar and feather him if he kept attacking slavery in his newspaper. Lovejoy was not willing to give up. He ordered a third printing press and hid it as soon as it arrived. The mobs attacked again. This time they killed Lovejoy. Then they broke up the press and threw it into the river.

The mobs silenced Lovejoy but that was not the end

of the slavery question. It was not the end of bloodshed over slavery. Soon the whole nation would struggle through a bitter time. The Civil War would settle this question once and for all.

DO YOU REMEMBER?

Words worth remembering

Match the word from the chapter with its meaning.

1. reservation
2. canal
3. reaper
4. capital
5. capitol

A. a machine for harvesting grain.
B. land set aside for Indians.
C. a manmade waterway.
D. a city that is the center of government.
E. a building housing the government.

People to remember

Fill in the blank with the name of the person or people listed in the WORD BANK that correctly completes each sentence.

6. _____ was ruler of France when Louisiana was named by LaSalle.

7. _____ brought slaves to Illinois to work in his lead mines.

8. _____ and _____ were the first Europeans to travel the Mississippi to the Gulf of Mexico.

9. _____ signed a law saying colonists could not settle west of the Appalachian Mountains.

10. _____ led a small army in the Revolutionary War that fought and held forts in Illinois and Indiana.

11. A _____ is a group of disorderly people.

12. A _____ makes and repairs iron tools.

13. _____ invented a steel plow that made planting easier.

14. An _____ is the person in charge of a newspaper.

15. A _____ has the duty and power to make laws.

Word bank

editor

mob

LaSalle

King Louis

Deere

Renault

Clark

blacksmith

Tonti

legislator

King George

Think about it

Pick one of the people listed above, or someone else from this chapter, and write two diary entries for that person. One should be for a day filled with problems. The other entry should be written about a day filled with happiness.

Find out

Using a road map of Illinois, find the state capital, Springfield. What routes would you use if your family were going to visit the city? How many miles would the trip cover? What sites could you visit in the area of Springfield?

In your neighborhood

Pretend you are an explorer visiting your neighborhood for the first time. There are no streets, houses, or automobiles. The streets are really rivers and creeks. The buildings are mountains. The automobiles are buffalo. Everything else you see are natural things. Make a map showing the route from school to someplace near the school. Label the things on your map. Pass your map to a classmate and see if he or she can name where you are going.

CHAPTER

4

A Time of Troubles

Battle Cry of Freedom

Words and Music:
George F. Root

Spirited

1. Yes we'll rally 'round the flag, boys, we'll rally once a-gain,
Shouting the battle cry of Freedom, We will rally from the hillside, we'll gather from the plain, Shouting the battle cry of Freedom.

Chorus
The Union forever, Hurrah, boys, Hurrah! Down with the traitor, Up with the star; While we rally round the flag, boys, Rally once a-gain, Shouting the battle cry of Freedom.

This cartoon shows the "uncomfortable seat" Lincoln would have as the new president.

This black Civil War soldier may have served from Illinois. His name is not known.

A slave family being sold at an auction in New Orleans.

LESSON 1

Illinois: Slave or Free?

In Chapter 3 you learned of a man being killed because he spoke against slavery. He was killed over a question that divided our country. The feelings of Americans about slavery depended on where they lived. Those in the South generally favored slavery. Northerners were generally against it.

The South—slavery as a way of life

In the South, slavery touched everyone. First, of course, were the slaves. They had little power to make choices about their own lives.

Most slaves lived on large sugar or cotton *plantations*. From sunrise to sunset, everything they did was for the plantation owner. The kind of work they did depended on the time of the year. When there was cotton to be picked, a slave's day would go something like this:

A slave's day

The *overseer* had the slaves out of their huts and ready for the fields as soon as the sun came up. They wouldn't be back until well after dark.

The slave's day was spent picking cotton. It was back-breaking work. For hours the slaves bent over the cotton plants. Only the overseer could give the order to take a break. When it was time for a lunch of cold bacon, work stopped for five or ten minutes. Then it was time to pick more cotton. Often the overseer speeded up the slower workers with his whip. When it finally got too dark to see in the fields, it was time to weigh the cotton and do other chores. Wood needed cutting. Tools needed fixing. Animals had to be taken care of. The slave's day was not over yet.

By late in the evening, the slaves could prepare their suppers. Pork was heated over a wood fire. Cornmeal was

"Selling a Mother from her Child" is from the *American Anti-Slavery Almanac* for 1840.

This picture shows how slaves were hunted down by slave catchers.

These southern slaves are being watched by their overseer.

baked at the same time. Supper ended another hard day. As they went to sleep, the workers dreamed of the rest day coming up. Maybe the master would write a pass to let a slave or two visit the next plantation.

The slaves lived through each day with fear. They feared having their cotton weighed. If any slave had not picked enough cotton, he or she would surely be whipped. If a slave picked more than expected, there was another problem. The master might expect that much again the next day.

Slaves lived with another fear. They could be sold at any time. Members of the same family might be sold to people in different states. They might never see each other again. Even a slave with no family feared being sold to someone more cruel.

Slavery and southern whites

Three out of four southern whites had no slaves. They were mostly poor families with small farms. But they, too, were affected by slavery. Rich sugar and cotton planters with 50 to 100 or more slaves set the style for life in the South. Their slaves were a measure of their success. Many other southern whites looked up to this small group of slave owners.

Plantation owners with many slaves could become very wealthy. Land for growing cotton was not expensive. If the slaves worked hard, there was plenty of cotton to sell. This cotton was sold to clothes manufacturers in many countries. Plantation owners could make enough money to buy more land. They built beautiful plantation homes. And many owners could buy large homes in cities near the Atlantic Ocean or Gulf of Mexico. Living near the water was cooler than on the plantations during the summer.

Life in the North

Slavery was not important in the North. Farms in the North were not as large as in the South. Farm families had to work hard. But most could handle the farm work by themselves. Feeding and housing slaves would be too expensive for northern farmers. And when the steel plow and the reaper became widely used, planting and harvesting improved without adding more workers.

Besides, there were more jobs off the farm in the North than in the South. Thousands worked in factories. Workers were also needed to build canals and railroads. Other northerners worked for themselves making barrels, wagons, and other things for the home or farm.

Life was hard for factory workers in Illinois and other northern states. They, too, worked hard for long hours with few breaks. Unlike slaves, northern workers could be fired when they were not needed. No employer paid people who were too old or too sick to work. They had to feed themselves and their families as best they could while looking for work. But there was an important difference between northern workers and slaves. Northern workers were free. No one could whip them for not getting enough work done. No one would sell their wives or children and take them away.

Can the states live together?

Factories and free workers were important in the North. Slavery and cotton were important in the South. For years the people of the North and South lived with their differences. Two things changed this.

First, the government of the United States passed a law about returning runaway slaves. It said that runaway slaves were to be captured and returned to their owners. Those who captured slaves would collect money. Some people in Illinois caught blacks, free or runaway, and sent them to the South as slaves. Other Illinoisans became part of the Underground Railroad. They helped runaway slaves escape to Canada.

The Underground Railroad was not really a railroad. It was a secret way for slaves to escape to freedom. The word *underground* meant that it was hidden from slave catchers. The homes of people who hid runaway slaves were called *stations*. People who helped slaves from station to station were called *conductors*. The Underground Railroad helped 75,000 slaves escape to freedom over several years.

The Underground Railroad had stations through the North all the way to Canada. There were many here in Illinois. One was in Princeton. It was the home of a preacher named Owen Lovejoy. He was the brother of Elijah Lovejoy, who had been killed for writing against

Blacks leaving their cabin to begin a trip on the Underground Railroad.

slavery. Like his brother Elijah, Owen Lovejoy was an *abolitionist.* Abolitionists were people who worked to abolish, or end, slavery everywhere in the United States. Lovejoy had a fifteen-room house with many closets. In the days of the Underground Railroad, these closets hid many escaping slaves. When night came, the slaves would

HARRIET TUBMAN

Harriet Tubman was a runaway slave. In 1850 she heard that her sister's family had run away from their master. Tubman found them in Baltimore, Maryland. During the nights, the grownups took turns carrying the sleeping children. By day, the Underground Railroad hid them. Finally the small group reached Philadelphia, Pennsylvania. Harriet Tubman had completed the first of many trips she would make as a conductor on the Underground Railroad.

hide under a pile of hay on a wagon. Then Lovejoy would drive them to the next Underground Railroad station.

Lincoln and Douglas debate

Another thing bothered people in northern and southern states. It was the question of slavery in the *territories*. After all, the territories would someday be states. People everywhere argued about it. In 1858 two Illinois men *debated* the question. One was Stephen A. Douglas, an Illinois *senator* running for *re-election*. Douglas was a short man whom people called the Little Giant. People all over the country knew him. If Douglas won the debates, he would surely be picked to run for president of the United States in the next election.

Hoping to take Douglas's job as senator was Abraham Lincoln. Honest Abe was a lawyer in Illinois. Few people outside the state knew Lincoln. No one knew how important he was to become.

Lincoln and Douglas represented the ideas of people all over Illinois. Lincoln felt that slavery was evil. It should not be allowed to spread. "The real issue," he said, was the "struggle between right and wrong." Douglas said Lincoln was trying to start a war. "Let the people speak!" Douglas said. He believed the white people of each territory should decide if they wanted to own slaves.

The day of a debate was more fun than a carnival. Brass bands played and cannons boomed. Thousands of people came from nearby towns and farms. Picnics and games filled the day. Then the crowds gathered to hear Lincoln and Douglas debate.

Seven times, these two great men debated the slavery question. In Alton, Charleston, Freeport, Galesburg, Jonesboro, Ottawa, and Quincy they met. On election day, Senator Stephen A. Douglas was re-elected.

The battle wasn't over. Lincoln was now known all over the country. Two years later, he and Douglas met again. This time each wanted to be president of the United States. In November 1860 Abraham Lincoln was elected our 16th president.

LESSON 2

Artist's view of a Lincoln and Douglas debate. How is this different from a debate between two candidates for office today?

Who Was Abraham Lincoln?

Abraham Lincoln had not always lived in Illinois. He was born in 1809 in Kentucky. He lived there for the first seven years of his life. Like their neighbors, the Lincolns lived in a log cabin on a small farm.

In 1816 the Lincolns moved. They left Kentucky for two reasons. First, Abraham's father, Thomas, lost his farm. He decided to go where he could buy land and be sure he owned it. The second reason was slavery. Kentucky was a slave state. Thomas Lincoln did not believe in owning slaves.

So Thomas, his wife Nancy, Abraham and his sister, Sarah, moved to Indiana. The land they settled was covered with forest. Abraham Lincoln was large and strong for a seven-year-old. He helped his father clear the forest and build a new log cabin. Here Abraham Lincoln lived until he was 21 years old.

Abraham Lincoln was born in this cabin on February 12, 1809.

There was always plenty to do. But there was not much time for education. When there was time, there was not always a school open. Books and paper, too, were hard to find. Lincoln, like other children of his time, did his lessons on a smooth board. He wrote with a piece of charcoal. Lincoln went to several different schools for short times. In all, he spent no more than a year in school. Still, Abraham Lincoln learned to read, write, and work with numbers.

As a teenager, Lincoln became well known where he lived. While still young, he reached his full height of six feet, four inches. He was strong and a good worker. This made him a favorite among other farm families. Whenever he could be spared from his father's farm, he could work for his neighbors. His ability as a speaker also gained him attention. People liked to hear him tell stories.

Lincoln comes to Illinois

In 1830 the Lincolns moved to Illinois. Life had been hard for them in Indiana, and they had heard of the rich soil in Illinois. They bought a farm near Decatur. Again Abraham helped his family get started on their new farm. A year later, Lincoln began life on his own. He was hired by a boat owner to help take a flatboat to New Orleans.

This New Salem store where Lincoln worked is now a United States Post Office.

One of Lincoln's first jobs away from his family's farm was on a flatboat carrying goods to New Orleans.

The owner was pleased with Lincoln's work. He hired Lincoln to work in a store in New Salem. When he was not busy, Lincoln spent time reading and studying. He borrowed books and talked with people passing through New Salem to learn as much as he could. Being honest, brave, and friendly, Lincoln quickly made many friends. He also earned the nickname "Honest Abe."

Lincoln worked at three different jobs over the next two years. With a friend, he bought and ran a store. But in a few months the store failed. It took several years for Lincoln to pay off everyone he and his partner owed. Then he took a job as postmaster at New Salem. It earned him $30 a year. He also learned *surveying.*

In 1834 Lincoln won his first election. He was elected a representative to the Illinois General Assembly. The General Assembly makes laws for the state. It has been said that Lincoln was too poor to pay for a ride to the capital. According to the story, he once walked almost 100 miles from his home in New Salem to the state capitol in Vandalia.

As a representative, Lincoln made his first speeches against slavery. This was the beginning of a new life. He was elected three times to the General Assembly. During this time, Lincoln also became a lawyer. In 1842 he married Mary Todd.

Again and again, Lincoln spoke out against slavery. Then in 1858, his debates with Stephen A. Douglas began. They brought him to the attention of the whole country. And as you know, Abraham Lincoln became the first Illinoisan to be elected president.

LESSON 3

The Civil War

Slavery had been the main question in the race for president. In the South, people even spoke of taking their states out of the Union. They said they would form their own nation if Lincoln won. He did win. Before the end of the year, South Carolina left the Union. In the next six weeks, Mississippi, Florida, Alabama, Georgia, Louisiana, and Texas also withdrew. Abraham Lincoln had not yet taken office, and already seven states had separated themselves from the Union. They called themselves the Confederate States of America.

In March 1861 Abraham Lincoln took office as president. People all over the country waited to see what he would do. In his first speech, he said he did not plan to change the South. He would not try to end slavery where it was already allowed. He also said he did not plan to fight. War would not come unless the South started it.

And start they did! They had already taken over most U.S. government forts in the seven Confederate States. Lincoln did not try to get them back. But he said he would not give up any forts he still held.

Fort Sumter in South Carolina was one of the forts Lincoln refused to give up. Confederate soldiers fired on the fort. The fort's *commander* fought back. With only about a hundred soldiers, he held the fort for two days. By then the fort was on fire. The soldiers were out of food and ammunition. No one on either side was killed, but the South had just won the first battle in the Civil War.

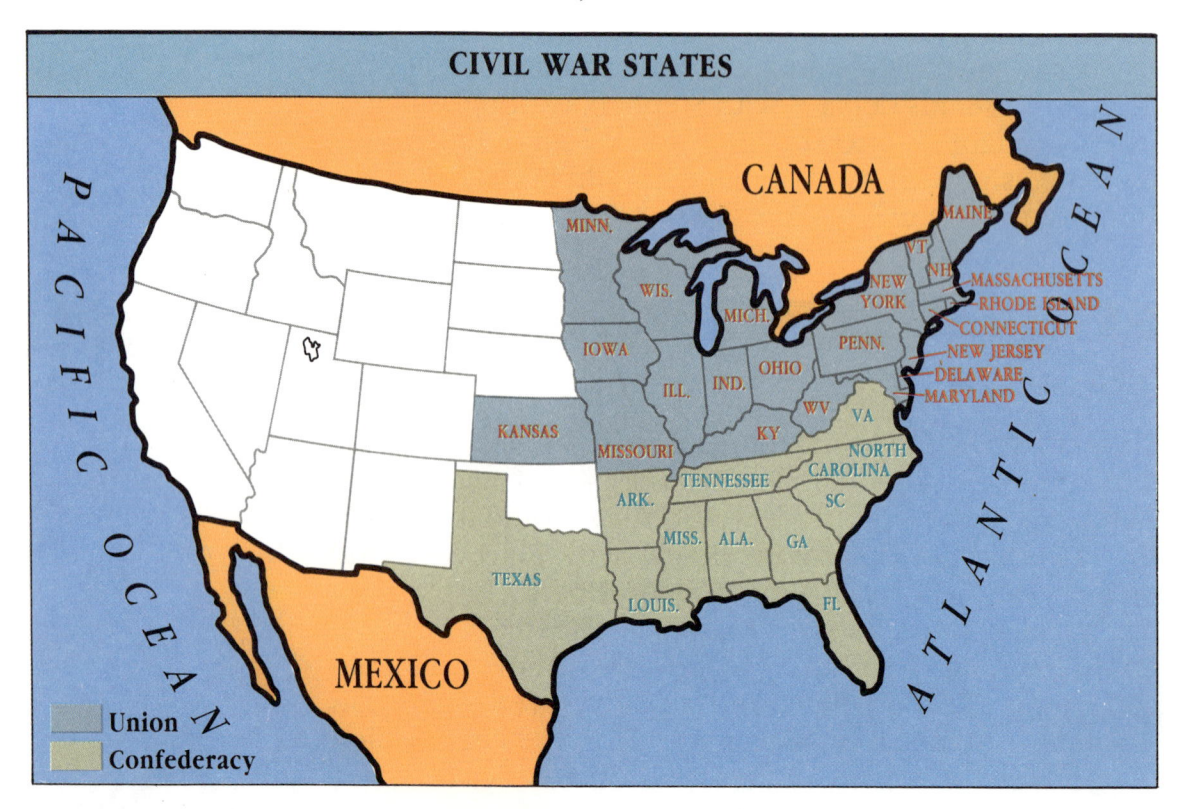

Lincoln asked for *volunteers* to help defend the Union. The rush of young men from Illinois was greater than anyone had expected. Sometimes whole groups of people like teachers, firemen, or lead miners signed up together. At first, blacks were not allowed in the army. But in 1863 they were allowed to join. About 1,800 blacks from Illinois went to war to save the Union. And women dressed as men to become spies or go into battle. Men and women from all parts of Illinois helped lead the Union to victory.

WAR SONGS

During the Civil War, a Chicago man named George F. Root wrote several war songs. Union soldiers sang his songs around campfires and on the field of battle. Songs like *A Battle Cry Of Freedom* (Rally Round The Flag) helped keep spirits up. War songs helped in another way. Hearing soldiers singing often discouraged those on the other side.

Men and women belong to groups which act out Civil War adventures today.

As the war began, southern states that were still in the Union had to choose sides. Four more states joined the Confederacy—Virginia, Tennessee, Arkansas, and North Carolina. Four slave states stayed in the Union. These were Delaware, Maryland, Kentucky, and Missouri. In all, 22 states remained in the Union. Eleven joined the Confederacy.

The war goes on

Both sides thought the war would be short. In the South, soldiers were asked to serve no more than a year. Lincoln asked for even less. He called for 75,000 soldiers to serve for three months.

But the war went on. And as it got longer, fewer soldiers signed up. Both sides had to *draft* men in order to get enough soldiers. Governor Richard Yates of Illinois helped. Yates was the soldiers' friend. He told the Illinois soldiers they would not be forgotten. He kept his word. Again and again, Yates visited hospitals and war camps to lift the soldiers' spirits.

The soldiers had other very important friends. Women helped set up hospitals, made bandages, and raised money. Mary Bickerdyke of Galesburg, Illinois, became famous for her service in the war. Mrs. Bickerdyke had been a nurse. She offered to help in the hospital at Cairo. She ended up traveling to 19 major battles with the soldiers. She gave first aid in the field and ran kitchens and hospitals. She set up the first army laundries. No longer would the clothes and bedding of wounded soldiers have to be burned. Not until the last Illinois soldier had returned home did Mrs. Bickerdyke leave the army.

Freeing the slaves

At first Lincoln said that the war was being fought only to keep the United States together. Owning slaves was wrong, he said. Yet his goal was not to end this evil. In some places, slaves left their homes and walked out to

Mary Bickerdyke served her country as a nurse during the Civil War.

Black soldiers served in the Union Army during the Civil War.

the fields of battle. Northern officers turned them away. They were not fighting to free the slaves.

For a year and a half, Lincoln held to this view. He offered to pay slave owners for any slaves they would free. Not one state took his offer. Lincoln had even asked the Confederate States to come back into the Union without freeing their slaves. They refused. Finally, in January

1863, Lincoln issued the Emancipation Proclamation. In it he said that all slaves in states fighting against the Union were free. Now the war took on new meaning. Northern soldiers were fighting to save people from the evil of slavery.

A long war

The Civil War was not short. At first the South won many battles. But the North was better able to fight a long war. The Union had more than three times as many people as there were free people in the South. And people in the North did not have to worry about slaves turning against them.

The North had more industry. Factories switched over to making things that were needed for war. And much was needed.

Northern farmers fed the army even with many farmers fighting in the war. There were few shortages of food for soldiers or the people back home. Illinois led the country in growing both corn and wheat.

The North had another advantage. Transportation was better. It had more than twice as many miles of railroad as the South. The railroads in Illinois were kept busy. They moved soldiers, food, and supplies to where they were needed.

Over four long years, Americans fought one another. Finally, on 9 April 1865, the South *surrendered.* The Civil War was over. The North had won, and the states were joined together again. Many soldiers in both armies had remembered they were fighting against other Americans. General Ulysses S. Grant, from Galena, Illinois, was a good example. A Confederate soldier described Grant's kindness at the end of the war's final battle: "He seemed more [willing] to feed his prisoners from the [food] of his own men than he was to [guard] his captives."

Over a half million men and women lost their lives in the Civil War. Almost 260,000 Illinoisans were soldiers or nurses. A New England author wrote these lines, prais-

ULYSSES SIMPSON GRANT

One volunteer who answered Lincoln's call was Ulysses S. Grant. He was working in a store in Galena when the war started. Because he had been a soldier before, he quickly became a leader. After winning many battles, Lincoln made him commander of the whole Union army. Grant's success as a general helped him become president of the United States in 1868.

General Ulysses S. Grant before a Civil War battle.

A HERO AROUND THE WORLD

He never left the United States. Yet, all over the world, his is the most honored American name. More books have been written in foreign languages about Abraham Lincoln than any other American. Many foreign artists have painted Lincoln's portrait. Some have changed his features to make him look like he was from their own country. And statues of Lincoln can be found on every continent in the world.

This drawing from the *National Police Gazette* shows Booth shooting Lincoln in Ford's Theatre.

ing our state for its part in the war:

> The prayer that springs in every heart,
>
> God bless thee, Illinois.

In 1865 Lincoln was elected again as president. He made it clear that he wanted to "bind up the nation's wounds," and to bring about "a just and lasting peace." As early as 1863, he talked of *pardons* for Confederate soldiers. He would ask only that they promise to follow the laws of the United States.

Abraham Lincoln never had a chance to serve as a peacetime president. Just five days after the war ended, he was shot. John Wilkes Booth, an actor, shot Lincoln in a Washington, D.C., theater. The next morning the president was dead.

DO YOU REMEMBER?

Words worth remembering

Match the word from the chapter with its meaning.

1. draft
2. pardon
3. surrender
4. volunteer
5. debate

A. to give up
B. to forgive
C. to take part in a formal argument
D. to choose people to serve in the army
E. to offer to help

People to remember

Fill in the blank with the name of the person or people listed in the WORD BANK that correctly completes the sentence.

6. A _____ led slaves to freedom on the Underground Railroad.

7. An _____ was a hired man who was the slave's boss.

8. _____ debated Lincoln and worked to keep the Union together.
9. _____ served as nurses and dressed as men so they could help fight the Civil War.
10. South Carolina left the Union when _____ was elected president of the United States.
11. Five days after the end of the Civil War, Lincoln was shot by _____ .
12. After 1863 _____ were allowed to fight for the Union.
13. A _____ was a piece of property, owned by a master.
14. A person who spoke out against slavery was an _____ .
15. _____ was a general who led the Union to victory.

Word bank

Stephen Douglas	John Wilkes Booth
Women	slave
Abraham Lincoln	abolitionist
conductor	overseer
Ulysses S. Grant	blacks

Think about it

Compare the life of a slave and a poor white living in the North. Make two columns on your paper. Write SAME and DIFFERENT at the head of the columns. List ways the lives of these people were the same and different.

Find out

Find streets, parks, or buildings named after Lincoln, Douglas or Grant in your town or city. Look in an atlas to find places near and far named after these Illinoisans.

In your neighborhood

Did your town have an Underground Railroad station? Contact your local historical society or library to find out what was happening in your neighborhood during the time of the Civil War.

82

CHAPTER

5

Growing and Changing: Chicago Case Study

Poster inviting women to join the army during World War I.

This alley in a tenement neighborhood shows how poorly many immigrant families lived. Some neighborhoods have continued to decline over the years.

View of Chicago in 1820.

People fled from Chicago just ahead of the flames.

Chicago, 1834. This row of houses may include two kinds—log cabins and balloon frames. Can you tell which is which?

COURTESY CHICAGO HISTORICAL SOCIETY, ICHI-04701

LESSON 1

A Village to A City

From the beginning, Chicago was almost certain to become an important city. Its location had always been a busy one. For hundreds of years, Indians walked across this spot. They carried their canoes from Lake Michigan to the state's inland rivers. Later DuSable had built his trading post at Chicago. Traffic to and from the trading post was busy. Even after the Fort Dearborn Massacre, people returned to the mouth of the Chicago River. By 1833, 350 people lived in Chicago.

Chicago was also a good place to do business. Because Chicago was on Lake Michigan, goods made in Chicago could be sent to many markets by boat. The city's earliest factories used materials that came from nearby. Many businesses were connected to agriculture. Farm animals were easily brought to Chicago for *processing*. Chicago's meat-packing industry began with the Clybourne Company in 1829. They cut and prepared meat to be sent to butcher shops. Lumber mills sprang up to turn Wisconsin and Minnesota trees into lumber for building. Iron mills used iron ore from Minnesota and coal from southern Illinois to make iron for construction and tools. Cyrus McCormick built his farm tool factory in Chicago.

People came to find work. As the number of people grew, so did the need for goods and services. As businesses grew, the need for workers grew too. Growing Chicago needed better transportation. *Plank roads* and a canal helped. Transportation, materials, and workers led to more business and industries. In other words, growth led to more growth.

People coming to Chicago needed places to live. In 1833 a new way of building houses was started. Instead of making notches in timbers so they fit together, thinner boards were used and they were nailed together. A house could be built in days instead of months. This kind of *construction* is called balloon frame. It is still used today.

Growing pains

The building of homes kept up with the city's growth. But other things did not. In the 1830s and 1840s, Chicago had no sidewalks or *sewers*. Its streets were not paved. They were just grass and dirt. Such streets were dusty or muddy, depending on the weather. There were mud holes one after another. In rainy weather, the streets could not be used at all.

The trouble with Chicago was that it was low and flat. Water did not drain quickly enough from its streets. In 1855 the *city council* had a plan. It decided to raise the streets and sidewalks above the mud. After the streets were raised, the buildings had to be lifted up. This project took years to complete. And as the work was done,

LAND VALUES

Chicago's early growth was marked by skyrocketing land values. In 1832 a piece of land 80 feet by 100 feet was sold for $100. This same land, located at the corner of South Water Street and Clark Street, cost $3,000 in 1834. In 1835 it cost $15,000. Can you imagine what it would cost today?

Workers raise a hotel so new streets can be built above the old muddy ones.

people had to climb up or down several flights of stairs as they walked along a single sidewalk. But in the end, Chicago did raise itself out of the mud.

Later, the city began paving its streets with wood blocks. The blocks were dipped in tar and laid like bricks. The block streets were then covered with a layer of *pitch* and a gravel topping. After years of dodging mud holes, wagon drivers were thrilled to have smooth new roads. Clean drinking water was another problem Chicago solved. In 1839 a company built a *reservoir* to collect lake water for the city. Then pipes were made by drilling three-inch holes through the length of logs and laying the logs end to end. A pump pushed water through these pipes to all parts of the city. But is wasn't long before Chicago outgrew this system. A *crib* had to be built in Lake Michigan. Cleaner lake water was pumped through the city in new metal pipes.

TRAVELING CHICAGO'S STREETS

To warn drivers, people put up signs near the worst holes in Chicago's early streets. The signs carried messages such as "No bottom," "Man lost," "Wagon dropped through," and "Shortest route to China."

Chicago's drinking water improved when water cribs were built a few miles into Lake Michigan.

The age of railroads

In 1831 the first railroad line was built in New York. It was 17 miles long. The train could travel twice as fast as boats on a canal. All over the country, companies began laying track. By 1840 there were almost 3,000 miles of track in 21 states. Illinois was one of only four states without a railroad.

But railroads cost a lot of money. Because they were costly, railroad companies wanted help from government. Imagine the following discussion taking place in the Illinois legislature about 1840:

Mr. Somerville: "Think of the good a railroad could bring to our farmers and *craftsmen*. No longer would they have to sell to their neighbors for whatever they could get. They could sell to people far from their homes.

"A railroad would bring more factories to our state. Businesses would use a railroad to sell goods to people all over the country. And more factories would mean more *taxes* and more jobs. Can we refuse our state this much-needed income? I say we cannot.

"Also, a railroad would not freeze and become useless each winter. Nor would its path be limited. A railroad can be built to take the shortest routes. And speed! Imagine, gentlemen, goods being brought to us at a rate of 15 miles an hour!"

Swain: "Do not be taken in by the fancy ideas of our friend Mr. Somerville. Our state does not have millions of dollars to spend on the wild ideas of *speculators*. Let them raise their own money to test their dreams.

"What would happen once the road was built? Who could buy the 'iron horses' needed to use it? Certainly not the farmer or craftsman! The state would do the work. You, my friends, would pay for it. And a few rich merchants would use it.

"What we need, my friends, is a canal. Canals have already been proven. The Erie Canal has brought a lot of trade to New York. The state is being well paid for the money it spent. Let our state put its money on a sure thing—a canal."

Chicago can be thankful for both canal fever and the railroad boom. Illinois chose both. In 1836 the Illinois and Michigan Canal was started. Two years later, the first railroad track in the state was begun. Both took years to build. *Recruiters* were sent to New York to bring back workers. People came from both the eastern states and Europe to work on these projects. The 97-mile canal was finally opened in 1848.

Meanwhile, Illinois' first railroad was put into use in 1842. It ran 59 miles from Meredosia to Springfield. Early trains were far from comfortable. After one train trip, a traveler said: "If one were not locked up in a box with 50 or 60 tobacco chewers; and the engine and fire did not burn holes on one's clothes; and one were not in danger of being blown sky-high or knocked off the rails—it would be the perfect way to travel."

By the end of 1856, over 2,000 miles of track ran through Illinois. Railroads connected northern cities like Galena, Freeport, and Rock Island to southern cities like Alton, Centralia, and Cairo. These tracks passed through Quincy, Peoria, Springfield, and Bloomington. But much of the time, Chicago was their destination. From all directions, first waterways and now railroads led to Chicago.

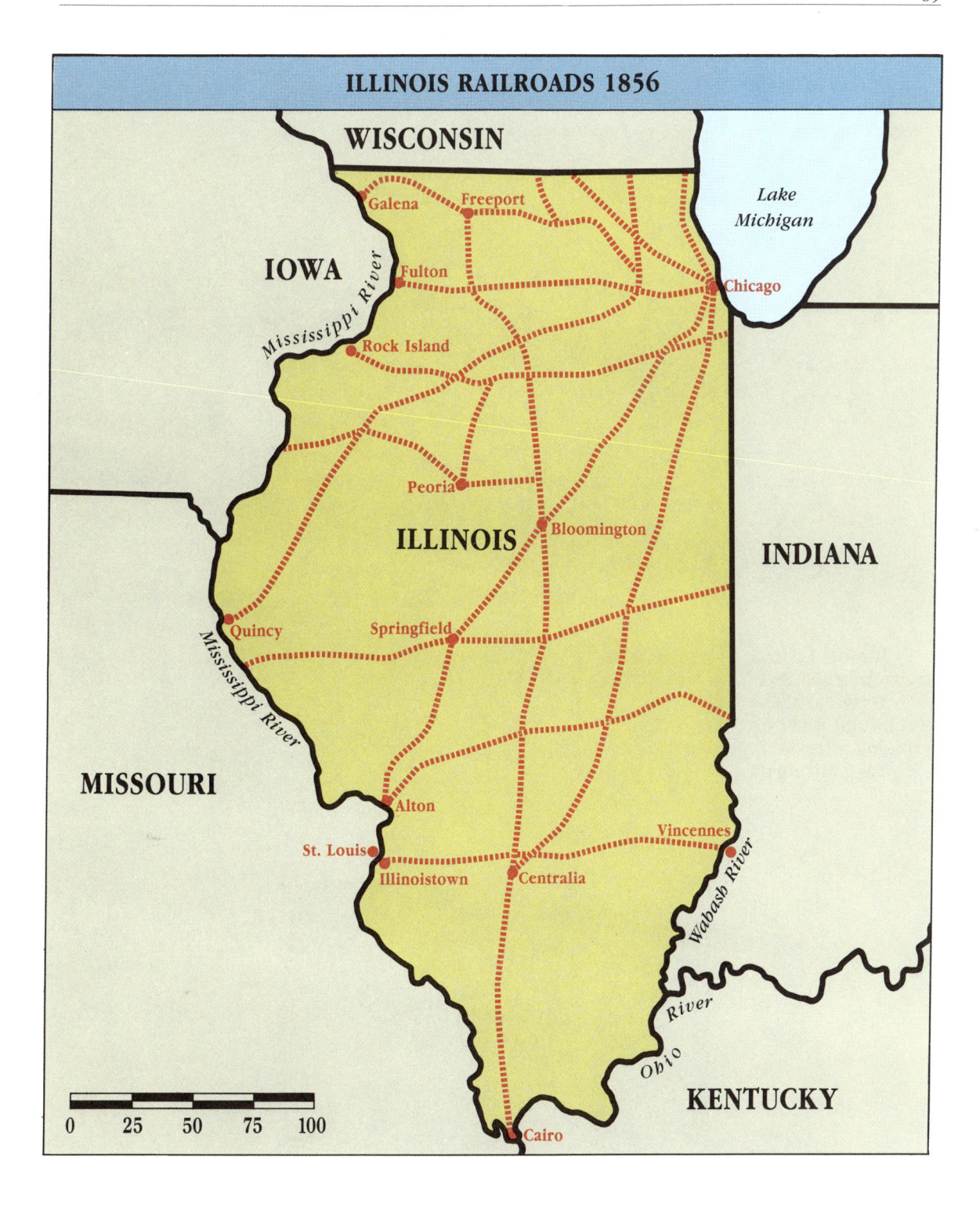

ILLINOIS RAILROADS 1856

A painting of workers laying Illinois Central tracks across the state. The artist is George I. Parrish, Jr.

COURTESY OF THE ILLINOIS STATE HISTORICAL LIBRARY

Illinois Central trains reached their terminal at the Chicago River by crossing a trestle in Lake Michigan.

COURTESY CHICAGO HISTORICAL SOCIETY

And like beads on a string, towns developed where the railroad ran.

Chicago became the world's largest railroad center. Over 100 passenger and freight trains entered or left the city every day. Eleven major railroads served the city. One of these was the Illinois Central—the world's longest railroad. Its 705 miles of track ran all the way from Chicago to the Gulf of Mexico. People and products from the north, south, east, and west passed through Chicago. Goods produced in and around Chicago could be shipped almost anywhere in the country.

Trains brought wheat and corn to the flour mills and grain elevators of Chicago. Soon it became the nation's most important grain market. By the 1880s the railroads had helped Chicago again. Using cars cooled by ice, fresh meat from Chicago could be sent to eastern cities. This meat was processed in Chicago's Union Stock Yards. The yards housed as many as 20,000 cattle, 75,000 hogs, and 20,000 sheep at one time. They were the home of companies like Swift, Armour, and Cudahy. Refrigerated railroad cars helped make Chicago the meat-packing capital of the world.

Trains also brought people to Chicago from eastern cities. Most of these newcomers were immigrants from Europe. By 1870, 300,000 people lived in Chicago. Half of them had come from other countries.

RIVERSIDE: A MODEL TOWN

Riverside was built along railroad tracks leading to Chicago. But it is not a typical *suburb*. It was designed by Fredrick Olmsted. Olmsted built New York City's Central Park. With William LeBaron Jenney, Olmsted planned a town with tree-lined streets that curved like the veins in a leaf. Almost half of Riverside's land was set aside for parks. Home owners had to plant trees to be sure their property was beautiful. Riverside became a model for other communities.

LESSON 2

The Great Chicago Fire

"A city of wood" is how Chicago in 1871 could be described. It had wooden houses and wooden barns with wooden roofs. Downtown business buildings up to six stories were built of wood. Sidewalks were made of wood. Even the streets were paved with wood blocks.

Imagine the city of wood after a long dry spell. Almost no rain had fallen on Chicago since the beginning of summer. Everything was dry. The stage was set for a terrible fire.

Tragedy began in a barn on DeKoven Street, a little south of downtown. The Patrick O'Leary family, who owned the property, had already gone to bed. *Legend* says that a cow kicked over a *lantern* and started the fire. No one knows what really happened. But Mrs. O'Leary's cow has become famous for starting the Great Chicago Fire.

Very soon the fire was out of control. Fanned by a strong wind from the south, the fire spread quickly toward downtown. Chicago's firemen were already weary from fighting fires the night before. Some of their fire equipment was no longer working. The firemen worked hard, but nothing helped—not even the Chicago River. During the night, the wind carried sparks and pieces of burning wood across the river. Downtown started to burn.

All Sunday night and all day Monday, the fire burned. At first people tried to save some of what they owned. But the fire spread too quickly. People ran to the lake and waded in. They stood in water up to their necks, afraid that they, too, might catch on fire.

The fire burned nearly everything in its path. By midnight on Monday, it had burned 35 blocks north of the O'Leary barn. There, with the help of rain, the fire was finally put out. More than 250 people had died. Over 90,000 people were without homes. Almost 18,000 build-

An artist's idea of how Mrs. O'Leary's cow started the Great Chicago Fire.

This view of Chicago's booming riverfront in 1866 shows a lumber company. What can you learn about life in the 1860s by studying this picture?

Men surveying the ruins of the 1871 Chicago fire.

ings had been destroyed. Amazingly, the O'Leary home was not burned.

During the fire thousands of people had taken trains out of the city. Those who had left, along with *telegraph* operators, soon spread news of the fire. From all over the country and around the world, people rushed to help. By the time the fire was out, help was pouring into the city. Trains began arriving with clothes, blankets, medicine, and cooked food. People also sent money. Almost $5,000,000 came from Americans and people in other countries.

Up from the ashes

Downtown Chicago and most of the north side of the city was in ashes. But all was not lost. Stock yards, grain elevators, and lumber yards on the south and west sides of the city were still working. And trains could still come into Chicago. The city's faith in itself was shown by *The*

Chicago Tribune. The newspaper's office had been destroyed. From a rented space, the newspaper came out the next day. It carried a story that gave hope to everyone. The message was clear. "CHEER UP! . . . CHICAGO SHALL RISE AGAIN!"

Chicagoans wanted to make sure fire could never again destroy their city. The city council outlawed wooden buildings downtown. By the end of the year, brick and stone buildings were already going up.

The fire gave young *architects* and business owners a chance to make a great name for their city. Many people who had lost their buildings built larger ones. One of these people was Potter Palmer, owner of the Palmer House. The new hotel he built on State Street became world famous. Palmer also sold land on State Street to merchants who wanted to rebuild their businesses. State Street became "that great street," Chicago's main shopping street.

There was work for everyone. Homes, apartment buildings, schools, churches, stores, factories, train stations, and bridges had to be built. Streets had to be paved. All the work to be done brought thousands of new workers to Chicago.

Kerfoot's real estate business opened the day after the Great Chicago Fire.

THE LOOP

To reduce street traffic, Chicagoans built tracks above the streets. First steam-powered trains and then electric trains were raised, or elevated. These elevated railroads were called "els." The el tracks formed a loop around the downtown area. Since that time, the center of the city has been called the "Loop."

Many Chicagoans built their new homes further from the center of the city. They could ride new cable cars to work. The fast cable car service is one reason Chicago's shape began to spread out.

Some people were afraid of the cable cars' speed. They raced through the streets at 8 miles an hour. But almost everyone liked the fact that these cars were not pulled by horses. They did not leave behind anything to clean up. Land values began to rise wherever cable cars went. Then in just ten years, they began to disappear. The cable cars were being replaced by electric trolley cars. The city also began to push upward. The need for more

Electric trolley cars moved people around Chicago and out to new suburbs.

THE LARGEST IN THE WORLD

The Sears Tower is the tallest building in the world. It reaches 1,454 feet into the sky. The tower has more than 16,000 windows which are washed by automatic machines 8 times each year. Rock pillars were sunk into the ground to hold up the tower. Each pillar is sunk as deep as the Statue of Liberty is tall. The building has a population of 12,000 people during each working day.

business space downtown caused people to build taller buildings. Three things helped buildings grow taller. First, better elevators allowed people to move around tall buildings safely. Then William Le Baron Jenney discovered how to make buildings extra tall. Using iron and steel skeletons to hold them up, Jenney began building skyscrapers! Along with a steel skeleton, skyscrapers depended on floating foundations. Because of Chicago's mud, heavy buildings sank and settled downward. By using large rafts under the buildings, huge skyscrapers could be built.

Jenney's steel skeleton is the foundation for gigantic buildings today.

View of buildings and main boat basin at the World's Columbian Exposition.

The Columbian Exposition

In 1890 Chicago began preparing to hold a world's fair. Only 19 years had passed since the fire. For the fair, beautiful white buildings were built along the lake front in Hyde Park. Each building was as beautiful as a palace. Each held wonderful *exhibits* showing changes in manufacturing, transportation, and the arts. In 1893 the fair opened. It was known as the World's Columbian Exposition. It celebrated Christopher Columbus' voyage to America.

People from all over the world visited the fair. They saw how new inventions could change their lives. The fair gave people a view of an exciting world to come. This was the first time electricity was used to light such a large area. Thousands of lights shining on the white "palaces" gave the fair the nickname White City. Later a stone copy was made of the fair's Fine Arts Building. It is Chicago's Museum of Science and Industry.

FERRIS WHEEL

Chicago needed a big attraction for its World's Columbian Exposition. George Ferris gave them what they wanted. He designed a wheel 264 feet high with 36 cars. Each car was 24 feet long, 13 feet wide, and 10 feet high. Forty people would ride inside each car and see the city from its windows.

LESSON 3

A City of Newcomers

Millions of people came to see the world's fair. Many also came from Europe and Asia to live in Chicago. Chicago grew from about a million people in 1890 to almost two million in 1900. Immigrants came looking for work. Most of them found it. Their work was sometimes hard and dangerous. Still, it was better than being poor and jobless in their homelands.

Large numbers of immigrants came for many years. The latest group of newcomers were often the poorest people in the city. They generally lived close to downtown. They moved into neighborhoods already crowded with others from their homeland. There the rent was cheapest. There they learned the language and ways of their new country. And after saving enough money, the children or grandchildren often moved away from these poor neighborhoods. New groups of poor immigrants then took their places in the older neighborhoods.

Growing pains

Growing so rapidly gave Chicago growing pains. The most crowded neighborhoods became *slums*. They got the worst care from the city and from *landlords*. The streets were dirty and poorly lit. Most were badly paved or not paved at all. Many houses were not connected to city sewers. And often garbage was not removed. Often the owners of these buildings refused to make needed repairs.

Slums and bad working conditions in factories became the target of *reformers*. They wanted to make life better for poor Chicagoans. One reformer was Dwight L. Moody. He spent much of his life bringing religion to poor people. He liked to help children. Moody helped build the first YMCA in the country.

Another Chicago reformer was Jane Addams. She was from Cedarville, Illinois. When she was 28 years old, Jane

Immigrants with little money lived in apartments like this one.

Dwight L. Moody in 1877.

Young boys learned the craft of making shoes at Hull House.

Girls learned to sew at Hull House. With this training a girl might get a job in a factory or a tailor's shop.

Addams visited a "settlement house" in England. Then she moved into one of Chicago's most crowded slums. There, she and Ellen Gates Starr started a home called Hull House. At Hull House they opened a kindergarten. They offered classes to help people learn how to live in America. Hull House was a place for people to meet and enjoy themselves. Here they could learn and sing and talk with their neighbors. Many immigrants took classes in English, child care, art, cooking, and sewing. The two women also started clubs for children and adults. Hull House made Chicago a happier place for newcomers. The idea caught on. People started settlement houses all over the country. In Chicago alone, 68 other homes have been opened.

Making the river run backwards

In the 1880s and 1890s, many Chicago children became ill. Many of them died. The trouble was the city's drinking water. Chicago got its drinking water from Lake Michigan. After heavy rains, city sewage ran into the Chicago River. Then the river carried it into the lake. As the city grew, it became very hard to keep lake water near Chicago clean enough to drink. After large amounts of river water ran into the lake, people would become ill.

Chicagoans found a way to help make their water safe. They dug the Sanitary and Ship Canal. It connected the Chicago River with the city of Lockport. The canal would be used by boats going between Lake Michigan and the Gulf of Mexico. It would also make the Chicago River run backward. Instead of flowing into Lake Michigan, the river now flowed toward Lockport. When sewage overflowed into the river, it now ran away from the lake. It flowed into the DesPlaines River. For eight years Chicagoans worked to dig the canal. Thousands of immigrants helped. Finally, in 1900, the canal was finished. Chicago again had clean, safe drinking water. But people living along the DesPlaines and Illinois Rivers were not very happy. They were sharing in Chicago's problem.

The tea room in Marshall Field's Department store, 1909.

Department stores and catalogs

Chicago is the home of the modern department store. It was started by Marshall Field. Field had owned a small store with Potter Palmer before the Chicago fire. After the fire, he reopened in a barn. But before long he was in a new building on State Street. Field stocked the best goods his buyers could find. There were furs, carpets, and the latest fashions. He also invited store owners in small towns to buy from his store. These owners could come to Chicago and pick out the items they wanted for their stores.

Field's was also famous for service to its customers. Shoppers were greeted by a doorman. The clerks were taught how to be friendly and helpful. Inside the store there was a library, children's playroom, restaurant, and telegraph office. Goods could even be delivered to the customer's home.

Mail order buying brought department store goods to villages and farms. The best at this business were Aaron Montgomery Ward and Richard Sears.

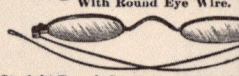

A person could order glasses from a Sears, Roebuck & Company catalog.

Ward arrived in Chicago at the age of 23. He worked for Marshall Field as a salesmen traveling to hundreds of small towns. Ward wondered why the same railroads taking him from place to place couldn't haul goods sold through a catalog. So he opened his mail-order business in 1872. It began with a one-page catalog of household goods. He soon became the "official" supplier for farm families all over the country.

Richard Sears was a telegraph operator in a small Minnesota town. During his free time, he sold odds and ends to friends in other towns. One day he bought pocket watches from a salesman. Sears told his friends at other railroad stations about the watches and let them be his salesmen. Within a few years, Sears was in Chicago running his new business.

Sears and Ward used catalogs instead of salespeople. It was cheaper that way. They filled their catalogs with drawings and descriptions. They explained clearly how people should measure themselves to order things that would fit. People could buy almost anything through the mail. Furs, eye glasses, medicines, wigs, cars, and even houses (lumber and plans) have been in the catalogs.

Look at the page from the 1900 Sears, Roebuck & Company catalog. Look at the instructions for ordering glasses. Use the chart to check your eyes.

Do you think a doctor would like you to order your glasses in this way? Do you think many people made mistakes ordering their glasses? How do you think people in small towns got glasses before they were offered in catalogs?

LESSON 4

Illinois in the Twentieth Century

The twentieth century opened with a war no one expected. The fighting involved so many countries it was called a "world war." On one side were the Central Powers. They included Germany and Austria-Hungary.

On the other side were England, France, Russia and the United States. They were the Allies. By its close, World War I would claim the lives of 10 million people.

Illinois goes to war

World War I started in Europe in 1915. The United States wanted to be *neutral*. But German submarines sank American ships. The United States joined the Allies in 1917.

Men from all over the United States came to Illinois. They trained at Camp Grant, near Rockford, to be soldiers. At the Great Lakes Naval Training Station, near Chicago, they became sailors. They learned to fly airplanes at bases near Belleville and Rantoul. Illinois itself supplied 300,000 men and women for military duty.

Illinoisans helped in other ways too. They bought *war bonds.* This gave the government money to use in the war effort. Boys from the cities helped farmers harvest their crops. Women made hospital supplies at Red Cross centers. They learned to cook without wheat or meat so these foods could be sent to Europe. Women went to work in factories making war supplies.

Volunteer groups at home helped support the army in many ways. Groups opened canteens for dances, donated food supplies to families at home, and trained women to work for the government, among other things.

> **EARLY RACE RIOT**
>
> Because so many men were soldiers, factories needed workers. Blacks from the South came to Illinois. They were paid lower wages than white workers. They were forced to live in overcrowded neighborhoods. White workers felt their wages were kept low because of black workers. Tension grew. Rioting broke out in East St. Louis. In Chicago, more rioting broke out after a black boy was killed for swimming at a "white" beach.

Illinois factories supplied the Allies. One in every three items produced in Illinois went toward winning the war. Steel was produced in Joliet and Chicago Heights. Peoria factories made farm equipment and steel wire. East St. Louis was a leader in making aluminum and animal feeds. Rockford and Moline factories made parts for machines. Alton manufactured brass for bullets. Guns were tested and stored at Rock Island.

The war had destroyed many of Europe's farms. Citizens as well as soldiers needed food and other farm products. Illinois farmers stepped up their production. Crop production in 1918 was the third largest in Illinois history.

After the war

The war ended in November 1918. Americans returned from Europe and wanted to forget the war. People who had lived with shortages wanted to live well now. Factories stopped making war materials and produced *consumer goods.* People wanted the new products they saw in the store windows. One of the most popular products was the automobile.

For $400 a person could own a Ford. But there were few paved roads to drive it on. Most roads were just paths made by a horse-drawn scraper. When the weather was dry, people choked on the dust. When it rained, horses had to pull the cars through the mud. It wasn't until 1927 that Illinois put a small tax on gasoline to pay for new and better roads.

Illinoisans even tried their hand at building cars. Hieronymous A. Mueller of Decatur was one of the first. But his effort ended in disaster. He was killed in an explosion while building his "Mueller" car. One hundred car companies went into business at different places in Illinois. None lasted very long. Dr. James Selkirk, of Aurora, built only one car.

Like the trolley and street car, the automobile changed where people lived. *Suburbs* boomed as paved roads spread out from cities. Many small towns stopped growing because farmers could travel into larger towns to shop. Can you think of other things that changed because of the automobile? Here are some hints: vacations, land alongside roads, jobs, insurance companies, sports, movement of products.

These flapper dresses were in style in the 1920s. This was the first time American women had worn dresses above the knee!

The Roaring Twenties

Americans chose to have fun during the 1920s. They took part in *fads*. There were goldfish-swallowing contests and marathon dances. Couples danced the Charleston. People bought new products like the radio and refrigerator. They listened to the new sounds of jazz by Louis Armstrong, Bessie Smith, "Duke" Ellington and "Jelly Roll" Morton. One hundred million people went to the movies each week. For the first time people went to sporting events in large numbers. Athletes like "Red" Grange, the "Galloping Ghost" of the Chicago Bears, and Babe Ruth became heroes.

The 1920s were also a time of crime and violence. A big reason was *liquor*. In 1920 liquor was outlawed in the United States. Those who still wanted to drink went to "speakeasies." Here they could buy liquor supplied by criminals like Al Capone. "Bootlegging" became big business. Gangs fought other gangs to keep their whiskey businesses. Often innocent people were killed in "wars" between rival gangs.

The depression

The Roaring Twenties came to an end in October 1929. That's when the stock market crashed.

During the 1920s business was booming. People had jobs and wanted to spend their money. Stores began to give *credit* so people could "buy now and pay later." Americans also bought *stocks* in companies with the hope of making more money. Banks bought stocks too. Stocks were often sold on credit. Everyone believed the roar of the twenties would go on for a long time.

It didn't! Farmers felt the *depression* first. After World War I American farmers continued to harvest record crops. But Europeans were farming again as well. And there were no longer armies to feed. With large amounts of farm products and fewer buyers, prices went down. Farmers who had borrowed money to buy equipment and seeds couldn't pay their bills. They lost their farms.

THE STOCK MARKET CRASH

People bought stock to make money. It worked this way. Suppose you bought stock in a business in 1928, when it was $150 a share. In 1929 it was worth $181 a share. This means people were willing to pay you $181 for each share you bought in 1928. If you sold your shares, you would make $31 for each share you owned. Here is what happened, instead, to stocks at the beginning of the Great Depression.

	Price in 1929	Price in 1932
Sears, Roebuck	$181	$10
General Motors	$ 92	$ 8
General Electric	$403	$ 9

People looking for work were a common sight during the Great Depression.

Buying of radios, cars, and washing machines also slowed down. Businesses had goods they couldn't sell. They stopped work and sent workers home. Without pay checks, workers couldn't spend as before. More businesses slowed down. People without work couldn't pay for the things they bought on credit. They couldn't pay their banks. Banks couldn't pay for stocks they bought. Then the stock market crashed. Banks closed because they ran out of money. People lost their life savings. The stock market crash marked the start of the Great Depression.

People lost their jobs and their savings during the depression. Family members tried to help each other. Friends tried to help friends. But there was little they could do. One in four workers was without a job. Men sold apples on street corners to earn some money. People stood in "bread lines" to get soup and bread handouts.

In Washington, D.C., the government decided to take action. President Franklin Roosevelt had a plan called the New Deal. Giant projects were started to create jobs. The government hired people to do the work. Dams were built to make electricity for farm communities. Highways and streets were repaired. New courthouses and schools were built. Parks were fixed up. Farmers were given loans to stay in business. President Roosevelt wanted people to start working again.

Another world war

The new programs helped. But it took another war to end the depression altogether. On 7 December 1941 Japanese planes attacked the United States naval base at Pearl Harbor, Hawaii. The United States was in World War II.

Sixteen million American soldiers, sailors and flyers fought in the war. They joined French, English, Russian, Canadian, and Australian troops in battle against Germany and Japan. As in World War I, Illinois was a leader in the war effort.

One million Illinoisans joined the armed forces. They and other Americans were trained again at bases like Great Lakes and Camp Grant. And because a large army had to be trained quickly, hotels and parks in Chicago were turned into *barracks* and training fields. Chicago also opened a USO club for servicemen and servicewomen. People in the military could drop into the club at any time. They could use the showers, game rooms, library and cafeteria for free! The building was especially crowded during weekend dances.

Again, Illinois' factories and farms went into high gear. The largest factory in the world was built in Chicago to make airplane engines. Huge plants opened in Rockford, Rock Island, Peoria, Springfield, Decatur and East St. Louis. Illinois even made boats for the navy. They were built on the Illinois River and floated to New Orleans. *Radar* was manufactured at the Western Elec-

Does your family album have pictures of men or women in World War II uniforms?

tric Company in Cicero. Over one billion pounds of explosives were produced at a plant near Kankakee.

Farms produced record crops. Illinois led the nation in soybeans. It was second in cheese, hogs, and corn. Illinois farmers combined better seeds with fertilizer in the rich prairie soil. The combination produced food for Americans at home, in the military, and people in other countries.

Illinoisans at home took part, too. They saved goods through a *ration* plan. Gasoline, sugar, rubber boots, coffee, and meats could only be bought with ration coupons. After meals, fats were collected for use in factories. People all over Illinois planted "victory gardens" to grow their own vegetables.

When the war ended in 1945, Illinois was proud of its effort. Sadly, it would again be asked to supply men and women for the armed forces during the fighting in Korea and Vietnam.

DO YOU REMEMBER?

Words worth remembering

Where shall I put it? Match the items with the correct location.

1. corn
2. cattle
3. aluminum
4. goods waiting to be sold
5. bootlegging

A. East St. Louis
B. warehouse
C. grain elevator
D. stock yard
E. Roaring Twenties

Ideas to remember

Choose the ending that correctly finishes each sentence.

6. Settlement houses (A. decided who was right in an argument, B. helped immigrants learn about life in a new land, C. seldom had sewers and garbage pickup).

7. The Great Chicago Fire (A. destroyed downtown Chicago, B. burned down Patrick O'Leary's home, C. burned itself out when it reached the Chicago River).

8. After World War I, people wanted to (A. get rid of automobiles, B. buy consumer goods, C. visit the Columbian Exposition).

9. Chicago solved its drinking water problems by (A. drilling larger holes in logs and laying them end to end, B. pumping water for drinking from the Chicago River, C. reversing the flow of the Chicago River).

10. During the depression, people (A. lost their jobs and savings, B. bought large numbers of refrigerators and automobiles, C. bought new farm machinery).

11. Because the value of land got very high in downtown Chicago, (A. stores went out of business, B. buildings got taller, C. buildings sat empty because no one could afford them).

12. Chicago had to raise itself out of the mud because (A. it is located in such a rainy climate, B. of the Chicago Fire, C. it was built on such low, flat land).

13. Illinois factories made airplane engines and radar for (A. use in World War II, B. sale in department stores, C. use during the Roaring Twenties).

14. Reformers wanted to (A. build slums, B. change Chicago's boundaries, C. make life better for the poor).

Think about it

If you were a reformer in your city, what would concern you most? Write a letter to the editor of your local paper voicing your concerns. Suggest solutions for your city's problems.

The automobile and airplane became very popular after World War I. Which of these two inventions has changed our lives the most? Explain your answer.

Find out

Use an encyclopedia to complete one of these projects. Remember to use the key words.

* Make a drawing to show how radar works.

* Make a model of a skyscraper showing its steel skeleton.

* Make a list of sports or movie stars from the 1920s and 1930s.

In your neighborhood

How would you travel from your home to Chicago's Loop? How many different methods of transportation could you use? How long would each take? How much would each cost? Put your answers on a chart with these headings:

TODAY'S TRANSPORTATION CHOICES TO CHICAGO'S LOOP

METHOD   TIME   COST

Collect family pictures of the World War II years and display them in the classroom with captions.

CHAPTER 6

Illinois Government

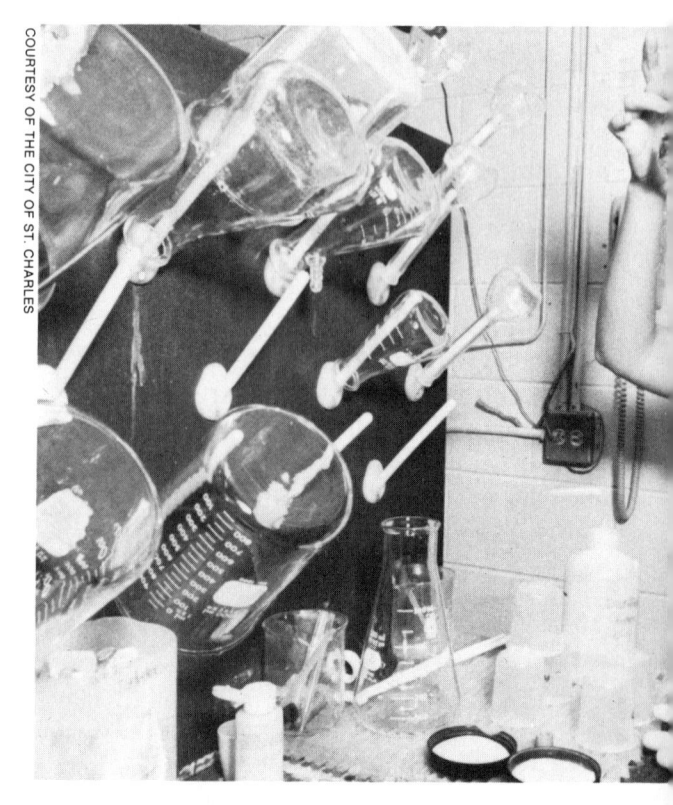

This woman works for city government. She is testing water in St. Charles.

Fireman from Geneva.

Local governments pay to have sewer lines put in place and repaired.

Entrance to the governor's office in the state capitol building.

LESSON 1

Our State and Our Nation

Over 200 years ago, when our country first became *independent,* Americans worried about rules. They felt a powerful government might treat them harshly. So when the states met to write a *constitution,* they gave the government of the United States only certain powers. Other powers were given to the states. The people kept important *rights* for themselves.

The United States Constitution joins all our states into one *nation.* It also tells what the government in Washington, D.C., can make rules about. For one thing, the national government can make rules about buying and selling between people in different states. It can also coin money and run post offices. The Constitution gives the national government the power to make agreements with other countries. It expects the government to defend the United States in times of trouble.

United States Capitol, Washington, D.C.

The president runs the executive branch from the White House.

BRANCHES OF GOVERNMENT

EXECUTIVE
Carries out the laws

LEGISLATIVE
Makes the laws

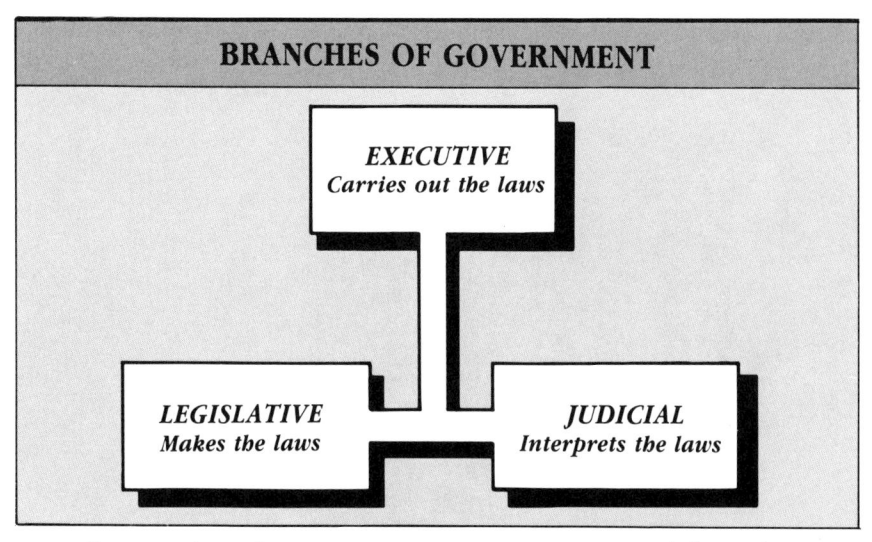

JUDICIAL
Interprets the laws

Our national government protects people's rights. In the United States, people have the right to attend the church they wish. They may freely write and talk about their ideas. They can meet together to talk about things that bother them. If a person is arrested for breaking a *law,* he or she must be treated fairly. The people even have the power to make changes in the Constitution itself. These changes are called *amendments.*

The Constitution divides the job of government among three branches. These are the *executive, legislative,* and *judicial.* Each branch has certain duties and may not do the work of any other branch. This keeps the power of government spread out so no branch becomes too powerful.

The president is the head of the executive branch. The president makes sure that the laws of the national government are carried out. The legislative branch is called Congress. Congress is made up of two houses: the Senate and the House of Representatives. The people in each state *elect* senators and representatives to be a part of Congress. Senators and representatives meet to make laws which all states must follow. *Courts* make up the judicial branch of government. The courts settle arguments about what the constitution and laws really mean.

Illinois has laws about cleanliness on dairy farms.

Government in Illinois

Our country is made up of fifty states. Each state is like the others in some ways and yet each is different. Because they are different, each state must deal with different problems. To do this, each state has its own state government.

States have the power to make laws for their own needs. Arizona makes laws about how water can be used. Water is very important because Arizona is a desert state with less water than it needs. California inspects food entering the state. It wants to protect California crops from insects that might be brought in with a load of fruit or vegetables. Wisconsin makes laws about fishing in its many lakes and rivers. Louisiana has laws about safety on the docks where ships load their cargoes. West Virginia makes laws about safety in its coal mines. Illinois makes laws about cleanliness on dairy farms.

Illinois has a constitution which tells how state government will work. Our first constitution was written in 1818, when Illinois became a state. As Illinois grew

OUR STATE CAPITALS

Illinois lawmakers met in Kaskaskia for two years. In 1820 Vandalia became the state capital. When the walls, ceilings, and floors of the capitol building began to crumble, Illinois looked for a new capital. Nine lawmakers from Sangamon County helped convince the legislature to move to Springfield. (The Sangamon legislators were called the Long Nine because of their height.) In 1839, thanks to the work of Abraham Lincoln and his eight tall friends, Springfield became the capital of Illinois.

This capitol at Vandalia was built to try to stop Springfield from becoming the new capital of Illinois.

and changed, new constitutions were written. Over the years, there have been four different plans for our state government. Our present constitution was passed by the people of Illinois in 1970.

State executive branch

Like the Constitution of the United States, our state constitution divides government into three branches. The governor is the head of the executive branch and is elected by the people of Illinois. It is the governor's duty to be sure state laws are carried out. Many people help the governor in the executive branch. Some are needed to collect tax money so the state can buy goods and provide services. Others help people get licenses to drive automobiles and run businesses. Workers in this branch help farmers market their products. They inspect farm animals to be sure they are healthly. Other workers plan and build roads. Still others help children without parents, work in state parks, and find jobs for people out of work.

Illinois State Capitol at Springfield.

Shadrach Bond was the first governor of Illinois.

BECOMING GOVERNOR OR A MEMBER OF THE GENERAL ASSEMBLY

To become governor or a member of the General Assembly in Illinois, you must win an election. But before you can run in an election, you must be an American citizen and . . .

Governor:

Be at least 25 years old and live in Illinois for 3 years.

If elected, a governor serves 4 years before facing another election.

Senator or Representative:

Be at least 21 years old and live 2 years in the part of the state you will represent.

If elected, a senator serves 4 years and a representative 2 years before facing another election.

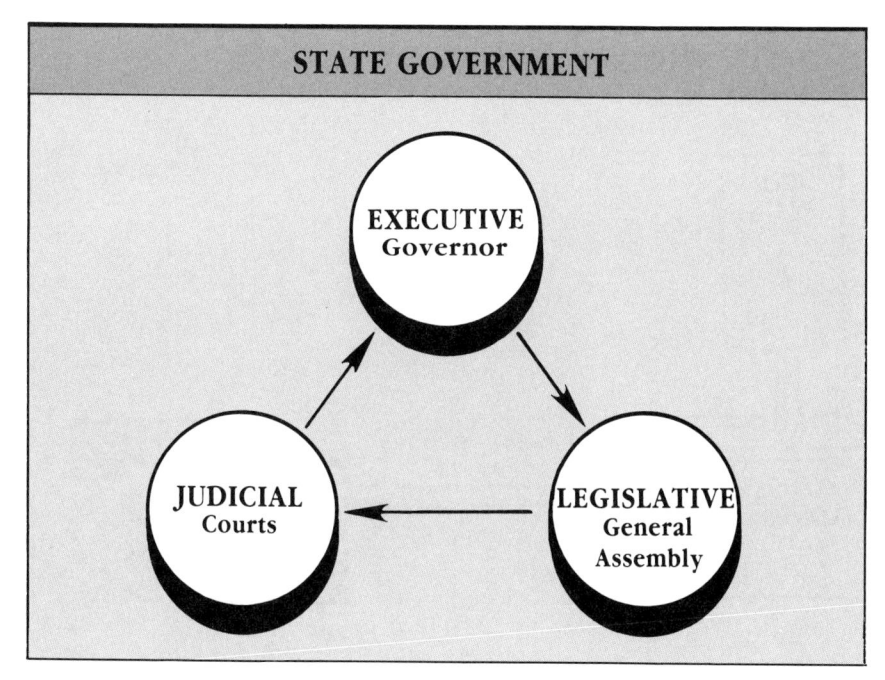

STATE GOVERNMENT

- EXECUTIVE — Governor
- JUDICIAL — Courts
- LEGISLATIVE — General Assembly

State legislature

Another branch of state government is the *legislature,* called the General Assembly. The General Assembly makes the laws for Illinois. It is made up of people elected to the house of representatives and the senate. The General Assembly meets each year to decide which *bills* become new laws. People from all over Illinois tell their legislators how they feel about problems by writing letters, calling on the telephone, and talking to them at their offices. Many laws start as ideas from citizens.

The way a bill becomes a law is shown on the chart on page 124. A bill can start in either the senate or house of representatives. The chart shows the path of a bill which started in the senate. After senators debate about the good and bad points of a bill, a vote is taken. If a *majority* of senators vote "yes" on the bill, it goes to the house of representatives. If a majority of representatives also vote "yes," it goes to the governor. If most of the representatives vote "no" on the bill, it goes no further. It does not become law.

HOW A BILL BECOMES LAW

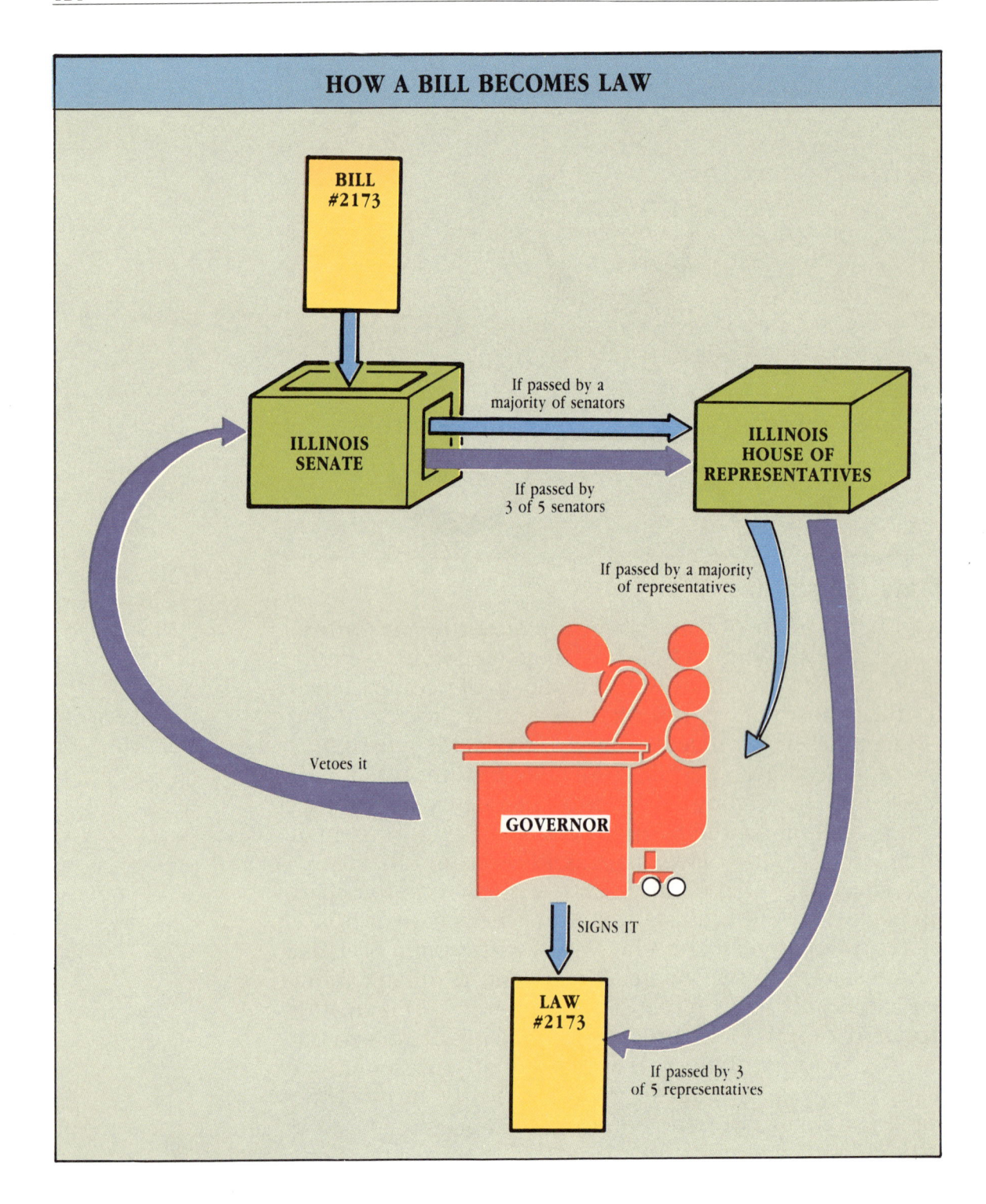

BILL #2173

ILLINOIS SENATE

If passed by a majority of senators →

If passed by 3 of 5 senators →

ILLINOIS HOUSE OF REPRESENTATIVES

If passed by a majority of representatives ↓

GOVERNOR

Vetoes it

SIGNS IT ↓

LAW #2173

If passed by 3 of 5 representatives

Men and women in the General Assembly make laws for the people of Illinois.

If the governor believes the bill would make a good law, it is signed and becomes a new law for Illinois. If the governor does not believe the bill would make a good law, it is sent back to where it started. This is called a *veto*. The senate can then vote again. If three of every five senators vote "yes," the bill goes to the house of representatives. If three of every five representatives vote for the bill, it becomes a law without going to the governor again.

State judicial branch

The courts make up the third branch of our state's government. The judges who are in charge of these courts are elected by the people of Illinois. They study the constitution and the laws passed by the legislature. Courts decide who is right when people disagree on what a law means.

Sometimes courts are asked to decide if a person is guilty of a *crime*. The judge and often a *jury* listen to the reports of police officers. They listen to other people who might have been involved. After everyone has been heard, the jury must decide if the person on trial is guilty or not. The judge then decides how the guilty person should be punished.

Tax money pays for courts to settle arguments.

In another kind of case, a person might feel that he or she has not been treated fairly. This might happen when one person buys something, only to find it is broken. Or a person might ask the courts to decide who was to blame for an accident. The court will listen to both sides and then decide on a way to settle the argument.

LESSON 2

Local Government

Illinois is 385 miles long and 218 miles wide. In some places, farms cover the land. In other places, skyscrapers, stores, and highways leave little land visible. Because different places have different needs, communities are given power by the state to have their own governments. The governments of large and small communities are called *local* governments.

One form of local government is the *county*. Illinois is divided into 102 counties. Counties collect taxes. They provide a place for courts to meet. They record births, deaths, and marriages. The county sheriff patrols along country roads.

A full-page map of counties and county seats appears on page 175.

The local government which touches your life most is the *municipality*.

St. Charles: local government in action

Pioneers started St. Charles on the Fox River. They picked a place where Potawatomi, Sauk, and Fox Indians crossed the stream on their way to and from Lake Michigan. In 1850 the tiny settlement became a village. In 1874 it held a special vote and became a city. At that time, St. Charles picked its first mayor and city council.

Life was different in 1874 than it is today. Animals played an important part in the lives of almost everyone. People around St. Charles were dairy farmers. They kept cows for milking. They used horses for transportation and farm work. The city council had to make rules about animals. When farm animals began roaming through the city, an *ordinance* was passed by the city council. It said that cows, pigs, sheep, and horses had to be fenced in. Another ordinance said that no one could roll a hoop or fly a kite where nearby horses might get scared.

Over the years, other local governments have come into the lives of people living in St. Charles. A school district was set up so children would have good schools to attend. A park district was created so people could have beautiful parks and fun things to do.

If you walk through St. Charles, you will see how local government works. Follow the path on the next two pages. Discover how local government serves the people. Try to figure out if each service comes from the city of St. Charles, the school district, or the park district.

128

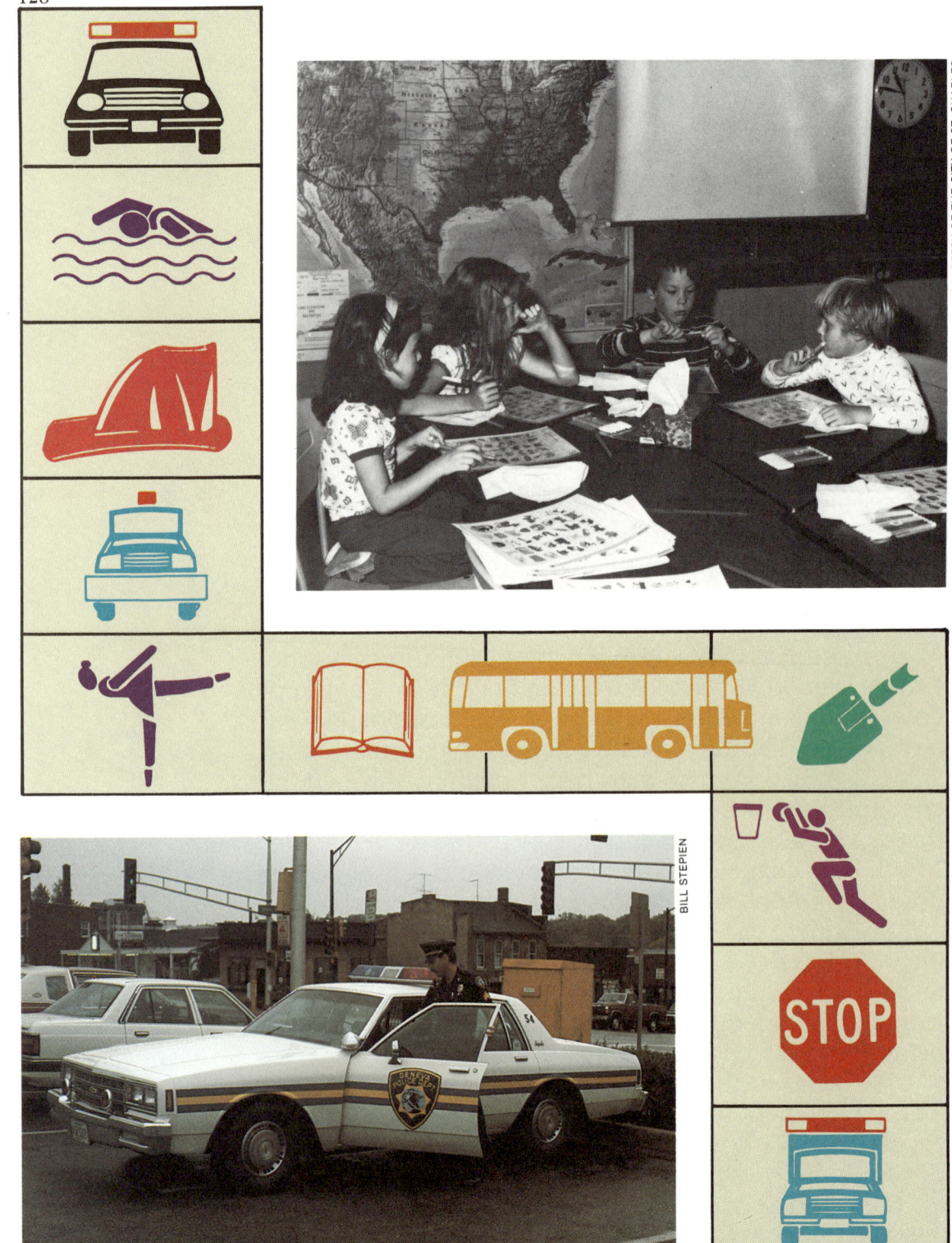

129

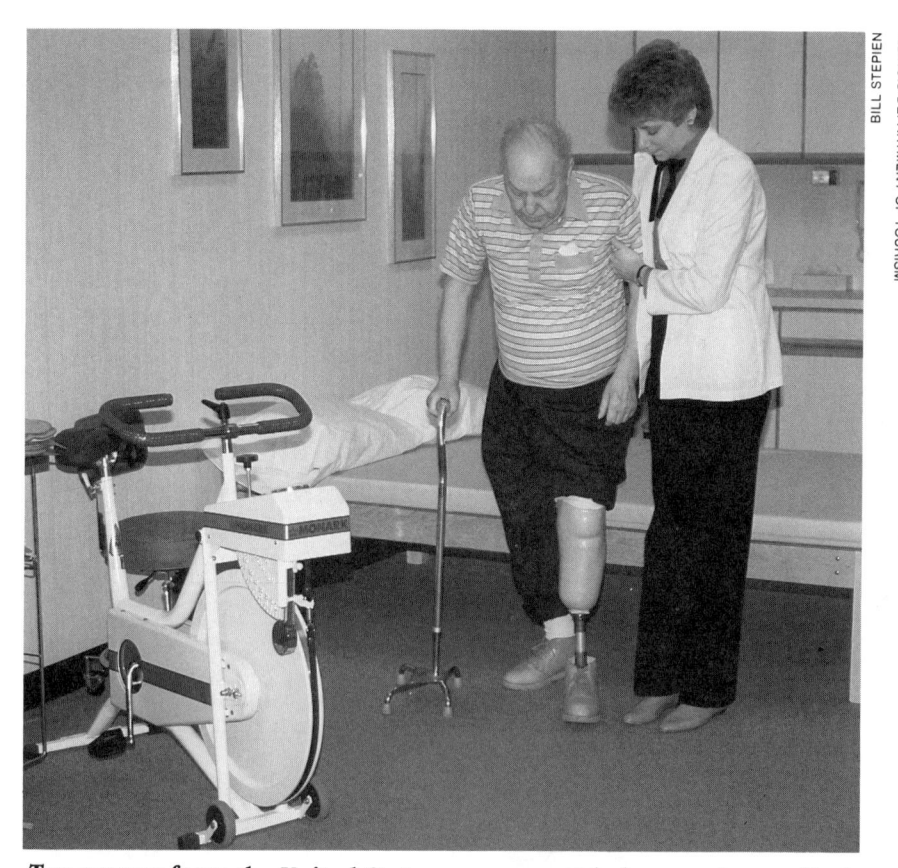

Tax money from the United States government helps pay for medical care for the elderly.

Tax moneys build and repair highways.

Taxes make things happen

Money for state and local governments comes in the form of taxes. Taxes are paid by the citizens and businesses of Illinois. Without taxes, people could not have the services you have just learned about.

Taxes come in many forms. Individuals and businesses pay taxes on their *income.* Those who have a large income are expected to pay more income tax than those who have a small income. When we buy things at stores and restaurants we pay a sales tax. Our license plate fees and highway tolls also are a kind of tax. Each county collects taxes on land, homes, apartment buildings, office buildings, and stores. These are called property taxes.

State parks, such as Lincoln's New Salem near Springfield, are helped with tax money.

Taxes are used to buy goods such as buildings, books, fire trucks, and office equipment. They also pay for the services of teachers, police officers, librarians, forest rangers, and other government workers. With the help of taxes, governments can make things happen.

You can see government working all around you. The next time it snows, watch government workers clear the streets near your home. When you enjoy a picnic in a state park, remember that land was set aside and kept beautiful with the help of state laws. As you travel across our country on a super highway, remember it was built with tax dollars collected by the government of the United States.

DO YOU REMEMBER?

Words to remember

Match the word from the chapter with its meaning.

1. constitution
2. amendment
3. bill
4. governor
5. legislature

A. an idea for a law
B. a change made in a constitution
C. written plan of government
D. makes the laws
E. carries out state laws

Ideas to remember

Decide whether each statement is true or false. Write TRUE if the statement is true. If it is false, rewrite the statement to make it true.

6. Our post office is run by our state government.
7. All states have different money systems.
8. Only the national government can declare war on another country.
9. Counties collect property taxes.
10. The courts settle arguments with the help of a jury.
11. People are hired to serve in the legislature.

12. The governor makes the laws for Illinois.

13. Our national government sends snow plows to clear the roads around our homes.

14. Our national government makes agreements with other countries.

15. People in all the states have the same problems.

Think about it

Find an article in your local newspaper about a problem facing local government. What is the problem? Who is involved? Why is this a problem? As a class, write a letter to the editor of the newspaper suggesting an answer to the problem.

Find out

Talk with a person who works in local government. Find out what his or her job is like. What things make the job difficult? When is the job interesting? Share your findings with your class.

In your neighborhood

Walk around the block at school or at home. Make a list of everything you see which is there because of a law. The law can be from the city or state government. Share your list with your class by drawing a picture of one thing from your list.

CHAPTER 7

Making A Living in Illinois

An automated television assembly line.

These boys are working the night shift in a glass factory.

Computers help people handle information of all kinds.

Modern dairy farming machinery keeps the milk clean. Milk goes from the cow, through pipes, to a holding tank.

The whole family pitched in with the work on Illinois dairy farms. Farm families in the 1860s tried to be self-sufficient.

135

This worker is building or repairing a house.

LESSON 1

Making Goods and Services

People want many *goods* and *services*. What they do to get these things is called "making a living." Working at a job helps us make a living. Work earns us money to buy what we want.

Sometimes ways of making a living change. Why do they change? There are several reasons. But they all have to do with the four *factors of production*.

Four factors of production

Four things are needed to produce goods and services. These are *natural resources, human resources, tools,* and *risk taking*. Natural resources are things we get from the earth, water, and air. For instance, trees can be used to build houses and furniture. Iron ore and coal are used to make steel. What natural resources are used for making hot dog buns, a pearl necklace, a sweatshirt, or a toy truck?

Human resources are also called *workers. Labor* is the work people do to make goods. Or labor can be used to produce services like teaching school or running an office.

We also need tools to make things. Tools are called *capital.* Plows, fishing nets, sewing machines, and money are all capital.

Finally, producing something to sell means taking a risk. A risk is taken by the people who start businesses. They risk their time and money in order to make a *profit.* Such people are called *entrepreneurs.* A barber or dentist who runs his or her own business is an entrepreneur. So is the owner of a factory or farm. A child who sells lemonade, mows lawns, or runs errands is an entrepreneur. All these people face the same risk. It might cost them more to produce their goods or services than they earn from selling them. In that case they do not make a profit. They suffer a loss. Without a profit, they cannot stay in business.

Working in early Illinois

Nine out of ten people in early Illinois made their living from farming. The natural resources are just right. Illinois has rich soil and a long growing season. The first farms were small. Most of a family's labor was needed to grow enough for themselves. There was little left over to sell. With little to sell, families had little money to hire helpers. Without much money, farmers could not buy tools. They had to make their own tools by hand. Sometimes there was no money at all. Then people traded their goods for the goods or services of someone else.

Farmers took a risk coming to Illinois. They had to use natural resources, tools, and labor wisely. If they didn't, they were in for hard times. And if the weather got bad, too, farmers could be "out of business."

Mining

Illinois has important natural resources called *minerals*. Most minerals are taken from the ground by mining. For a long time, lead mining was important in northwestern Illinois. Later, salt and then coal began to be mined in central and southern Illinois.

Salt was very important in the 1700s and 1800s. It was needed for more than just taste. Except in winter, meat had to be salted or smoked to keep it from spoiling. Salt was so important that Illinois allowed slave labor in southern Illinois salt mines. The slaves were rented from slave owners in Kentucky and Tennessee.

Here is how the salt was mined. Wells were dug from 30 to 80 feet deep. Salt from the ground dissolved in the well water. This salt water was pumped out of the ground and boiled in huge iron kettles. After the water boiled off, the salt could be scooped out.

Wood fires were needed to boil off the water. So the first salt wells were dug in places where there were plenty of trees. When the trees ran out, the kettles were moved to a new wood supply. Logs were hollowed out and joined together to pipe the salt water to the new place.

These men are checking a salt well.

Again and again the kettles were moved. After awhile, it became harder to find new sources of wood. But then coal was found near the salt mines. Coal fires were built.

Illinois salt mines stayed in business until the 1870s. At that time better salt wells were discovered in West Virginia. Illinois could not compete with West Virginia. In just a few more years the West Virginia mines closed, too. A new invention, the refrigerator, reduced the need for large amounts of salt.

Coal

You may remember from Chapter 1 that there is coal under two-thirds of Illinois. Around the time of the Civil War, coal mining became important. Coal was replacing wood as a fuel. It was burned to heat homes, heat iron ore for making steel, and to make steam for steam engines. It became the fuel of the railroads.

Coal mining, railroads, and iron making grew together. Iron ore could be made into iron and steel on top of a hot coal fire. But coal couldn't get to the factories until railroads connected the plants and mines. Mines couldn't grow until someone was willing to buy more coal. Railroads could grow if they had plenty of goods to carry. Can you see how the three fit together? The railroads connected factories with the coal mines. The mine owners sold plenty of coal. Factories had coal to make iron and steel. The railroads had coal and iron to carry.

The need for coal brought a need for mine workers. Owners hired young immigrants to work in the mines. By 1900 there were 100,000 people working in Illinois coal mines.

The miners worked long hours in poor conditions. Young boys and their fathers worked side by side. Sometimes they only saw daylight on Sundays. For their labor they received $1.50 a day. Meanwhile, the owners became rich. The price of coal jumped up as more and more factories used it for fuel.

Springfield coal miners had a dirty and often dangerous job.

"Breaker boys" were paid low wages to break large lumps of coal into smaller pieces.

To fight back, mine workers joined *unions*. Illinois miners joined the United Mine Workers. Like other workers, miners wanted safer working conditions, shorter workdays, and higher pay. Often the union workers went on *strike*. They refused to work until the owners agreed to treat them better.

Mine owners hired non-union workers to break the strikes. New immigrants were offered jobs. Black miners from the South could make more money in Illinois mines. Mine owners brought in trainloads of strike breakers. They hired armed guards to protect the trains. Strikers collected weapons of their own. Again and again fighting broke out.

UNION MINERS CEMETERY

A strike against low pay for coal miners began in 1897. Coal companies went to southern states to find miners willing to work during the strike. The miners were brought north on trains with armed guards. When they reached mines near Pana and Virden, strikers and guards both opened fire. Seven strikers and four guards were killed. The union miners were buried in the Union Miners Cemetery at Mount Olive. Unions still hold a memorial service at the cemetery each year.

Monument to union mine workers at Mt. Olive Cemetery.

COURTESY OF THE ILLINOIS STATE HISTORICAL LIBRARY

More strikes, more violence

Plenty of workers were ready to work in the factories. The workers came from other countries. They came from all over Illinois and other states. In the 1800s wages were low and the workday was long. Workers did not get extra pay for long hours. They didn't get paid for vacations. Their pay was cut when business got slow.

In 1873 business slowed down all over the United States. Railroad business was especially slow. Some railroads cut the workers' pay. The railroads argued they would go out of business if they didn't. Then the workers would have no jobs at all. Railroad unions began to strike.

The strikes stopped service on some Illinois railroads. Strikers blocked the railroads at East St. Louis, Peoria, Galesburg, and Decatur. The governor warned the strikers to go back to work. Then he asked the president of the United States for help. Soldiers were sent to the railroad stations, and the strikers left. The unions had lost, but

Newspaper picture of the strikers' fight at Virden.

they decided to grow stronger. They formed bigger, more powerful unions. Workers in *trades* joined the American Federation of Labor.

Trouble between unions and companies kept on. In 1886 a tragedy took place. The McCormick farm tool plant in Chicago cut the pay of its workers. There were strikes. On 4 May 1886 workers met in Haymarket Square. There were speeches against the company. Two people had been shot to death in front of the plant the night before. Just as the meeting was ending, police marched into the square. They ordered the people to leave. Someone in the crowd threw a bomb. It killed seven officers. The officers shot into the crowd. One more person was killed.

By the end of the summer, seven men were arrested for the bombing. There was a trial and each was found guilty. Some had not been in Haymarket Square when the bomb went off. Many people blamed unions for the angry times.

Police move into Haymarket Square.

COURTESY OF THE ILLINOIS STATE HISTORICAL LIBRARY

The John Deere factory in Moline, Illinois, around 1860.

LESSON 2

Industry Booms

You've already heard about two inventors who helped Illinois farmers. John Deere and Cyrus McCormick changed the way farmers made their living. These were entrepreneurs in the business of farm machines.

John Deere was a wealthy blacksmith. Remember that at first he made his plows by hand. When he could not make enough plows by himself, he hired workers. He added more capital in the form of tools. He gave up his work as a blacksmith to open a factory. Deere risked his time and money. He took a chance that farmers would buy his plows. If they did, he would make a profit and stay in business.

Cyrus McCormick gave up his home in Virginia to open a factory in Chicago. He took a chance when he moved to Illinois. How many reapers would he be able to sell? Could he sell them at a high enough price? He had to pay many workers. He had to buy materials and tools. He had to build a factory and pay other bills. He hoped to sell enough reapers at the right price to make a profit.

Agribusiness

The risks that Deere and McCormick took were good for them and for our state. They produced new tools that made important changes in farming. With them, farmers produced more food without adding more labor. Farming became a business. No longer did farm families grow crops just to feed themselves. They grew food chiefly for sale to others. They would now depend on others to supply them with what they didn't raise themselves. Farms became larger, and farmers began to *specialize*. Illinois farmers began to raise huge amounts of corn, soybeans, and hogs.

Farming has come to be called *agribusiness*. Farmers are no longer in business by themselves. They are now part of a food industry. Here's how it works. Farmers raise plants and animals for food and clothing. Railroad, trucking, and boat companies move the products to other companies. Meat packers make steaks, chops, lard, and other meat products. Mills make flour out of grain. Bakers buy flour for bread. Butchers buy meat for their stores. They advertise in the newspapers. Banks help keep the money going to the right people. People visit stores to buy bread, meat, and many other foods.

Buyers and sellers make deals for future sales of wheat, corn, soybeans, and other farm goods at the Chicago Board of Trade.

THE FOOD DOLLAR

This graph shows where each food dollar goes. What things might be in the category of "other"?

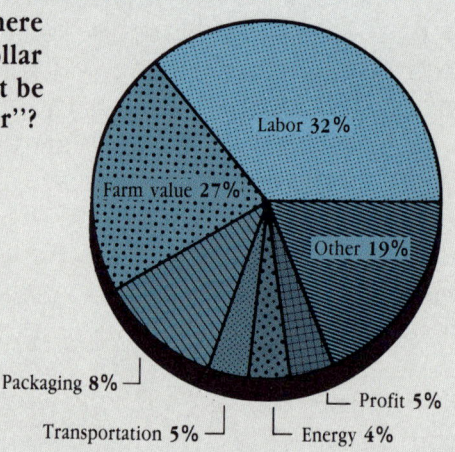

- Labor 32%
- Farm value 27%
- Other 19%
- Packaging 8%
- Transportation 5%
- Profit 5%
- Energy 4%

Source: U.S. Department of Agriculture

THE UNION STOCK YARDS

The Union Stock Yards in Chicago opened on Christmas Day 1865. Trains brought cattle, hogs and sheep to the yards. Here they were kept until processing at nearby packing houses. Then, in the 1870s, Swift and Armour started making refrigerated train cars for carrying meat. The Chicago Stock Yards became the world's busiest. Forty thousand workers processed 18,000,000 animals a year. Meat packing had become a "big business."

COURTESY OF THE ILLINOIS STATE HISTORICAL LIBRARY

Steel and railroads

Illinois entrepreneurs brought together natural resources, labor, and capital to make goods. Sometimes these things came from Illinois. Many times they came from nearby states. Steel is a good case study. At one time, steel had to be bought from England. Then Pennsylvania began to sell steel to Illinois factories. But entrepreneurs in Illinois saw a way to make money. Everything needed to make steel could be found in Illinois and nearby states. Iron ore could be shipped from Minnesota. Boats could carry it on Lake Michigan. Coal could be hauled by train from southern Illinois. There were plenty of workers in and around Chicago. In a short time, Illinois had climbed to the top in making steel.

George Pullman was an entrepreneur in the railroad business. His dream started with a sleeping car. He opened the Pullman Palace Car Company to make the railroad cars. Then George Pullman had another idea. He believed workers would be happier if they could live in a special town. The town would take care of all their needs. Pullman thought the town would make the workers better at their jobs.

The town of Pullman was started in 1880. Land was bought in the village of Hyde Park. Houses and apartments for 1,400 families were built. All were made of brick and had inside toilets. Besides the factory and homes, there were a shopping center, bank, and church. Pullman also built a school, library, fire station, theater, and hotel.

Pullman planned everything carefully. He used clay from the bottom of nearby Lake Calumet to make bricks. Steam from the factories helped heat the homes. Not even the town's sewage was wasted. It was made into fertilizer and used on a company farm outside the town. This farm supplied vegetables for sale to the people of Pullman.

Pullman's factory and his company town were a big success. But after a while, workers began to complain.

Soldiers helped end the Pullman strike. How would you describe what's happening in this picture?

They wanted to own their homes. They wanted a choice of where to live and shop. There were few choices to be made in the town of Pullman. George Pullman owned everything. A person could be born in a Pullman house, fed Pullman food, and go to a Pullman school. The same person could pray in the Pullman church and work in the Pullman factory. And when he died, he would even be buried in the Pullman cemetery.

Things got worse in 1894. Businesses lost money and had to fire workers. Many closed down. However, workers at Pullman didn't lose their jobs, but their pay was cut. The workers became very angry. Their pay had gone down, but rent and food prices stayed the same. Without other homes and stores near Pullman, workers were forced to pay Pullman's high prices. The workers went on strike.

It was long and violent. Railroad workers in other states joined the strike. When trains carrying United States mail could not get through strike lines, the president sent in soldiers to end the fighting. The strike didn't last much longer. Bitter workers went back to work at Pullman or left to find other jobs.

In 1898 Illinois courts ordered George Pullman to sell much of his town. One person would not be allowed to have so much power over workers. Most of the homes were sold to the workers who lived in them.

Many good jobs depend on a good education.

Service jobs grow

By the 1900s, more Illinoisans were working in factories than on farms. And work in service businesses was growing rapidly.

In early Illinois there were few service workers. Almost everyone was producing goods. Only a few people worked as store clerks, surveyors, lawyers, bankers or teachers. Then the growth of farming and industry helped bring about new service jobs. The banks grew to help businesses grow. Education became important to prepare people for more complicated jobs. Lawyers represented companies and people in business deals. Towns and cities began to offer more services to their citizens. Department stores were opened and mail order businesses were started. New household goods appeared in stores. With this growth came these kinds of service jobs:

store clerk	engineer	designer
architect	librarian	guard
firefighter	manager	bookkeeper
police officer	cook	teacher
mail carrier	salesperson	doctor
mechanic	secretary	nurse
bank teller	conductor	cashier

Managers make plans for how goods and services will be produced and sold.

Harvesting grain is much faster with modern machinery.

Photographers provide a service.

WORKERS IN ILLINOIS

This graph shows the number of workers in 1980 and the projected number for 1990.

Goods-Related Industries	1980		1,773,000 workers
	1990		1,660,000 workers
Service-Related Industries	1980		3,113,000 workers
	1990		3,375,000 workers
Farming	1980		115,000 workers
	1990		97,000 workers

= 200,000 workers

LESSON 3

Making A Living Today

When our state was young, almost everyone farmed. Out of every 100 Illinois workers, 80 helped raise food. By 1900 an Illinois farmer produced enough to feed 10 people. Today we have more people to feed. Yet, only 3 out of every 100 Illinoisans work on farms. A farmer today can feed more than 75 people.

Farming became big business in the late 1800s. Smaller farms were joined together to make large farms. Machines helped speed up planting and harvesting. More land could be cared for by fewer workers.

Workers then turned to *manufacturing* to make a living. By the 1960s, Chicago alone had a million workers in almost 15,000 factories.

Today another change has taken place. Illinois is still a leader in railroad equipment, soap, cans, glass, and automobile parts. It still leads in making electrical parts, radios, T.V.'s and telephones. But making a living in Illinois is changing again. Today less than 20 out of every 100 Illinois workers is in manufacturing.

Let's review for a second. Three of every 100 workers are on farms. Twenty of every 100 are in manufacturing. That adds up to 23 out of 100. What do the other 77 workers do? They produce services, not goods. And what has caused this change? *Technology.*

Technology is changing Illinois

Technology is the use of scientific knowledge in industry. Technology brings new tools and machines. Jobs are done in new ways. Scientists discover new ideas and put them to work. Workers in "high tech," or computer industries, produce information instead of goods. They service other people and machines. Generally, workers in high tech must have more education and training than workers in many other fields.

The growth of high tech

The age of high tech came to Illinois in 1945. During World War II, the United States brought together hundreds of scientists. They worked at the University of Chicago. Led by Dr. Enrico Fermi, they did secret experiments. The scientists found a way to split an atom. Atoms are the building blocks of all things. The splitting of one of these tiny atoms released a great deal of energy. Part of that energy could be used to split other atoms. It caused a chain reaction, setting off more and more energy. This is how the atomic age began.

Research leads the way to new products and ways of doing things.

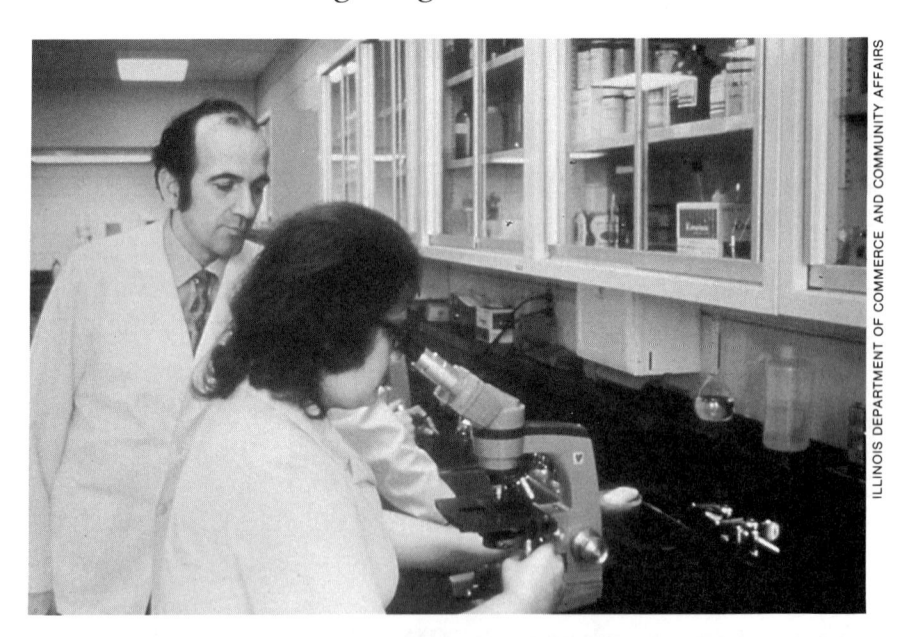

THE ATOMIC BOMB

While World War II was going on, a new weapon was being built. Using the discoveries made at the University of Chicago, the United States was the first to develop an atomic bomb. President Truman warned the Japanese to surrender or he would use the bomb. When they refused, one bomb was dropped on Hiroshima, Japan. Another was dropped on Nagasaki a few days later. The Japanese soon surrendered. Each bomb killed thousands and injured thousands more.

The experiments showed something else important. Bringing a number of brains together to study a problem leads to results. This is called *research*. Soon industries began to hire people just to do research. Many companies set up research laboratories in places away from their factories.

THE HIGH TECH CORRIDORS

Research centers are appearing throughout Illinois. But two areas seem to be magnets. Research centers are springing up along the Northwest Tollway—Interstate 90—between Chicago and Elgin. A second "high tech corridor" can be found along Illinois Route 5 between Oak Brook and Aurora.

High technology has come to most Illinois industries. Almost all use computers in one way or another. In some places, machines are run by computers. In others, computers write letters, answer phones, and check on the quality of work. In agribusiness, electronic microscopes and computers are used to develop new seeds. Many Illinois farmers have computers on their farms. Computers help keep the farmers' budgets in order. They even figure out the right foods to give hogs and other animals.

Have you ever thought of all the technology around you? Think about your local shopping center. To begin with, think of all the plastics in the building. They probably didn't even exist when the first atomic experiments were going on. Next think about the car or bus you ride to the shopping center. It was probably built by robot machines. The engine may be controlled by a computer. Maybe your car's radio can find a strong station by just the touch of a button. The cash registers in the stores are also high tech. They add up all the things you bought. Then they charge the correct tax. When the machines know how much money you gave the clerk, they figure your change. The machines even keep a record of what everyone bought that day.

Inventions come more quickly with the help of research. Computer-run machines are taking the place of some workers. This is called *automation*. Goods can be produced faster through automation. When this happens, the worker must train for a new job. Education is a service industry that helps train workers for new ways of making a living. Education is a key to new jobs in the future.

Look at the graph on page 150 comparing jobs in different industries. What will happen to the number of workers in goods and services? How will you likely earn a living in a few years?

DO YOU REMEMBER?

Words worth remembering

Match the word with its meaning.

1. capital
2. labor
3. natural resources
4. technology
5. entrepreneur

A. things we get from the earth
B. tools needed to produce goods
C. people needed to produce goods
D. use of scientific knowledge in industry
E. person taking a risk to make a profit

People to remember

Match the person with the correct description.

6. Enrico Fermi
7. strike breaker
8. Cyrus McCormick
9. George Pullman
10. John Deere

A. built a town for his workers
B. a person willing to work during a strike
C. his steel plow allowed farmers to plant more crops
D. helped split the atom
E. built his reaper factory in Illinois

Ideas to remember
Circle the word that best completes each sentence.

11. Wood and (coal, salt) were important fuels in early Illinois.

12. Before refrigerators, people used (coal, salt) to keep food from spoiling.

13. Another name for human resources is (labor, capital).

14. Today, (fewer, more) farmers than ever are needed to produce enough food.

15. (Automation, strike) is when machines take the place of workers.

Think about it
What would you need in order to become an entrepreneur? Plan your own business. Give your business a name. Make a list showing what you need to get started. It might look like this:

MARY'S LEMONADE STAND		
CAPITAL	**NATURAL RESOURCES**	**LABOR**
pitchers	lemons	Mary
spoons	water (ice)	Mary's brother?
glasses	sugar	Mom or Dad?
can opener		

Find out
In what ways is atomic energy used today? Use the encyclopedia in your search. Here are some keys words which can help you get started:
medicine   X rays   food processing   electricity

In your neighborhood
Use the yellow pages of your telephone directory. Look at the top of the pages for the key words which tell you what's on each page. Pick one key word for each letter in the alphabet, if possible. Make a list of the words. Next to each word (way of making a living), write "good" or "service," depending on what that business produces. Are the jobs in your community mostly in goods or services?

156

CHAPTER

8

Connected to the World

BILL STEPIEN

This satellite dish can bring programs from around the world to your television.

ILLINOIS DEPARTMENT OF TOURISM

View of Water Tower Place shopping center in Chicago.

157

A St. Patrick's Day parade takes place in Chicago every March.

This corn will be made into different products and sold around the world.

LESSON 1

People Connected to People

Can you remember some of the people who came to Illinois from other countries? They came to work on railroads, canals, skyscrapers, and farms. They worked as laborers, bosses, and secretaries. They became police officers, judges, teachers, and politicians. They brought with them ideas, skills, and customs.

Customs, food, and religion

You are connected to people by sharing their customs. St. Patrick is the patron saint of Ireland. The celebration of St. Patrick's Day was brought to Illinois by Irish settlers. Irish residents in Chicago have held a St. Patrick's Day parade every year since 1843. People wear green clothing whether they are Irish or not. The city has even dyed the Chicago River green. Have you ever worn green on St. Patrick's Day? You are sharing in a custom. You have connected yourself with people all over the world.

Chinese in Illinois celebrate special days, too. The Chinese New Year is a time for fireworks, parades, and parties. It is also the time for lion and dragon dancing. During the dragon dance, 50 people parade the dragon's 150-foot-long body through the streets. You have probably never been a part of a dragon dance. But there is another way to be connected with Chinese people. Eat Chinese food.

Chinese food can be found throughout Illinois. So can the food from many other countries. Are any of these familiar to you? Have you ever tried tacos, tostados, or chorizo sausage from Mexico? Maybe fish and chips and Yorkshire pudding from England is more to your taste. Or have you ever enjoyed blintzes in a Jewish restaurant? In many families, special foods have been passed along over the years. Does anyone in your family prepare cannoli (Italy), liver pate (France), schnitzel (Germany), or moussaka (Greece)?

ALL AMERICAN EATING

What's more American than hot dogs and apple pie? Actually, neither of these favorite foods got its start in America. Hot dogs began in Germany as frankfurters, named for the city of Frankfort. Pies got their start in ancient Greece. The Romans filled their pies with fruit. What's more American than hot dogs and apple pie? Probably roasted buffalo steaks and hominy.

Food from around the world can be found in Illinois.

THE WORLDLY SAUSAGE

Did you know that sausage was prepared and eaten by people as early as 1500 B.C.? The Romans called it "salsus." Sausages connect you with the world. Here's how.

Sausage	Country of Origin
Weiners	Austria
Bratwurst	Germany
Frankfurter	Germany
Black Pudding	England
Bologna	Italy
Pepperoni	Italy
Chorizo	Mexico
Plokworst	Netherlands
Szynkowa	Poland
Landjager	Switzerland

MOTHER CABRINI

Maria Francesca Cabrini was born in Italy. She was the thirteenth and youngest child in her family. She became a nun and came to the United States to work with Italian immigrants. In 1891 Mother Cabrini came to Chicago. She started hospitals, schools, and orphanages. People loved Mother Cabrini for her courage and work in helping others. She died in Chicago in 1917. In 1946 the Roman Catholic church named Mother Cabrini a saint.

Religion also connects Illinois with the world. Do you remember why French missionaries came to our state? Today Illinoisans are missionaries in many other countries. Your church or temple probably helps these people work in Asia, Africa, and Latin America. And church workers still come to Illinois! Father Peter Hung is a Catholic priest from Vietnam. He works in Chicago with people from Vietnam who are new to Illinois. Edwina Gately is from England. She helps homeless and troubled women in Chicago find food and shelter at Genesis House.

Religion connects us in another way. We share the

This nine-sided house of worship in Wilmette welcomes members of the Baha'i faith. Do you know where this religion began?

beliefs and customs of others. Our religions spread across states and other countries. When we travel, we can usually find people to worship with who believe as we do. Maybe you have met visitors from another country at your church or temple.

Travel connects us

"Travel." Does that remind you of ways Illinois is connected to the world? Thousands of Illinoisans travel each year. They travel to buy and sell. Travel can be for visiting friends or family members. Sometimes teachers and scientists travel to other countries to learn new ideas. And much of the time Illinoisans travel for fun. They go to islands in the Caribbean for warm weather and sandy beaches. They visit Egypt to see pyramids or Greece to see the ruins of ancient cities. Vacationers go to places which are interesting and fun. Vacationers from other countries come to Illinois for the same reasons.

Illinois is a very popular place. The Brookfield Zoo attracts people from around the world. So do the Lincoln sites in Springfield and New Salem. Thousands come to Chicago and visit the Art Institute, Adler Planetarium, and Shedd Aquarium. The box lists just a few of the places visitors come to see. When Illinoisans go traveling or visitors come to Illinois, connections take place.

ILLINOIS SITES TO SEE

There are hundreds of special places to visit in Illinois. Here are some favorites. Have you visited any of these places?

WHAT
Bishop Hill
Swedish pioneer life

WHERE
Bishop Hill

Brookfield Zoo
Cages without bars

Brookfield

Adler Planetarium See the stars	**Chicago**
Art Institute Famous art works	**Chicago**
Field Museum The earth's history	**Chicago**
Shedd Aquarium 10,000 water creatures	**Chicago**
Science and Industry Museum Exhibits work before your eyes	**Chicago**
Lincoln Park Conservatory The world's plants and flowers	**Chicago**
Grant's Home The general's home	**Galena**
Starved Rock State Park LaSalle's Fort St. Louis site	**LaSalle**
Morton Arboretum 4,000 plants line your walk	**Lisle**
Mormon Sites Original Mormon city	**Nauvoo**
Lincoln Sites New Salem village and Lincoln's home	**Petersburg/ Springfield**
Illinois State Museum Walk through Illinois history	**Springfield**
Cantigny Gardens and war museum	**Wheaton**

Boys and girls who play soccer are linking themselves with a tradition of Great Britain.

More connections

Stop and think again about ways you are connected with the world. Have you been bowling lately? Bowling was brought by Germans to America. Table tennis and badminton started in India. The Japanese introduced judo. Even baseball's roots can be found in another country. The English game of "rounders" probably led to American baseball. An Illinois team, the Chicago White Stockings, were champions of baseball when it began in 1876. And soccer goes back in history as far as any game. The Chinese were playing a game called Tsu Chu almost 2,500 years ago. Americans learned soccer from the English about the time of our Civil War.

There are even more connections. Musicians come to Illinois from all over the world. They study at Illinois schools. They perform with Illinois bands and *orchestras*. They can be seen at theaters throughout our state. Stores carry their records and tapes. We hear them on the radio and see them on television.

Illinoisans can see the work of world artists. We can watch movies made in other countries. Horses from Austria have performed in Illinois. So have *acrobats* from China and dancers from Mexico. Your newspaper tells when performers are visiting your area.

How many labels from countries of the world are hanging in your closet?

Illinois colleges train scientists, business people, teachers, and doctors from many countries. And guess what? Illinoisans visit other countries for the same reasons. The people of Illinois are connected with the people of the world.

LESSON 2

The World in Your Closet

Your closet is a good place to find connections to the world. Are there pajamas in your closet? Pajamas were invented in India. Do you have clothes made with silk? Silk was discovered in China thousands of years ago. The leather in your shoes is prepared in a way first used in ancient Egypt. The bright colors might have been seen first in Africa or South America.

Today's clothes are designed in many places. The idea for your new sweater might be from France, England, or Italy. The sweater itself could have been knitted almost anywhere. When you get home, check the labels in your closet. You'll probably find names like Mexico, Haiti,

India, and Poland. Be sure to check your shoes too. Look for countries like Italy, Korea, and Hong Kong. Clothes are often designed in one country and made in another. They are made with cloth produced in a third place from cotton or wool grown in a fourth. And how do the goods get from place to place? Probably on ships—ships built in Europe or Japan.

When clothes arrive in the United States, buyers look them over. Buyers represent stores like Sears, Wards, and Fields. Often they come to the Fashion Mart in Chicago. Inside the Mart, buyers try to pick clothes you will like. They hope you'll agree with their choices and make a purchase. When you buy, you are connecting yourself with many places in the world.

Made in Illinois

We are connected with the world through what we buy. We are also connected by what we sell.

Illinois is a manufacturing giant. We got that way for many reasons. First, materials were easy to get. Coal and oil were a short barge or train trip from manufacturing sites like Moline, Peoria, and Chicago. So were the raw materials needed for making iron and steel. Wood was available from nearby states. Second, trained workers were already in Illinois. Schools made sure young people learned the skills needed to do well on future jobs. Third, Illinois businesses used modern tools. The tools and newest ideas led to high quality goods. And lastly, Illinois had entrepreneurs. These were the people who could organize a business. They made the best use of materials, tools, and workers.

Illinois also became a giant because of transportation. Barges and boats still carry *cargoes* on Illinois rivers and the Great Lakes. Thousands of miles of railroad tracks crisscross the land. People and goods can move by railroad or truck throughout Illinois. In fact, they can go almost anywhere in North America.

Why is this barge on the Mississippi River important to Illinois' economy?

Hundreds of flights arrive at and leave from O'Hare Airport each day.

Getting to another country is not hard either. Large cargoes are floated down the Mississippi River to New Orleans. There they are loaded onto larger ships for their trip across an ocean. Or the cargoes can be sailed from the Port of Chicago on the Calumet River. These ships reach the Atlantic Ocean by way of the Great Lakes and St. Lawrence River. And, if you are in a hurry, there is O'Hare Airport. Many airlines use this airport, making it the busiest in the world.

Multinational companies

Some companies in Illinois have gotten so big they are called *multinational companies.* This means they have offices in other countries as well as the United States. CPC International in Argo, Schaumburg, and Danville is a good case. CPC makes products from corn. So it is easy to see why the company is in Illinois. Illinois is our country's second biggest corn growing state.

ILLINOIS MULTINATIONAL COMPANIES

Many Illinois companies do business overseas. These companies have plants or offices in other countries. Are any near your home?

CITY	COMPANY
North Chicago	Abbott Laboratories (medicines)
Northbrook	Allstate Insurance (insurance)
Chicago	Amoco Oil (refinery)
Chicago	Beatrice Foods (groceries)

Skokie	Brunswick Corporation (sporting goods)
Peoria	Caterpiller Tractor (tractors)
DeKalb	DeKalb Agresearch (agricultural products)
Moline	Deere and Company (equipment)
Glenview	Kraft Inc. (food)
Schaumburg	Motorola (radios)
Freeport	Newell Companies (hardware)
Skokie	G. D. Searle & Company (health products)
Chicago	Sears, Roebuck & Company (merchandise)
Decatur	A. E. Staley Manufacturing (corn/soybean products)
Oak Brook	Sunbeam Corporation (appliances)
Rockford	Sundstrand Corporation (aircraft parts)
Glenview	Zenith Radio Corporation (electronics)

How is CPC connected with the world? Let's take a look. CPC plants can be found in seven European countries. One thing they make is corn *starch*. It's used in batteries, soaps, crayons, paints, plastics, and rubber tires. And that's not all! Corn starch is also used in aspirin, baby foods, and beer. Also add to the list chocolate drink, pie filling, and chewing gum.

In South America we can find CPC plants in 8 more countries. Like other CPC plants, these make corn starch and *dextrose*. Dextrose is used in cookies, bread, and ice cream. It's also in jelly, peanut butter, and vinegar. If we went to Australia, Japan, India, or Pakistan we would find CPC plants. And they would be making the same products. Products from Illinois corn connect us with the world.

ILLINOIS FARM PRODUCTS GET AROUND

Illinois is first among all the states in selling farm goods. Here are the products it sells to other countries:

Soybeans and soybean products	**Cattle hides**
Corn and corn products	**Poultry and eggs**
Wheat and wheat flour	**Lard and tallow**
Barley, sorghum, and rye	**Milk products**
Meat (beef, pork, veal) and meat products	**Fruits and vegetables**

Here's a question for you: Who benefits from the sale of Illinois corn? Farmers? Correct! But who else benefits? Thousands of people who work in Illinois businesses. These are workers who turn corn into other products. The number includes scientists who develop better corn seeds. There are truck drivers who haul corn from fields to *grain elevators*. Workers making farm tools also gain. So do banks, railroads, and hundreds of other businesses.

Other goods leaving Illinois

Isn't it amazing how many people are connected to the world because of corn? Now think about this. Illinois also sends soybean, vegetable and meat products to other countries. More products, more connections!

Just one more thought about connections and Illinois

workers. Have you thought about the other goods shipped from Illinois? Here is a list of just a few. And remember, each is another link to the world.

Oil products	**Paper products**
Chemicals	**Books**
Office machines	**Fertilizer**
Parts for airplanes	**Farm machinery**
Scientific equipment	**Metals**
Medicines	**Furniture**
Parts for engines	**Hospital supplies**
Electric motors	

Goods enter Illinois

Being a giant doesn't mean Illinois has everything it needs. Illinois' climate and soil don't allow us to grow certain crops. To get them, we depend on other countries.

The Port of Chicago connects our state with the world.

COMING TO CHICAGO

Ships arrive at the Port of Chicago every month. Here are the places visited by ships coming to Chicago in just one month:

India	Yugoslavia	Norway	Peru
Turkey	Belgium	Senegal	Ecuador
Morocco	Germany	Togo	Guatemala
Italy	England	Nigeria	Colombia

Bananas connect us with Central and South America. So does the coffee bean. For chocolate we depend on countries in Africa and South America. That's where cocoa beans grow. Paper for bags and newspapers is sent to us from Canada. Natural rubber, tea, and many spices take us to Asia. For mums we depend on Colombia. Other fresh flowers come to Illinois from Thailand and the Netherlands.

When it comes to minerals, we connect again. Almost all our diamonds come from South Africa. With bauxite from Canada, South America, and Africa we can make aluminum. We depend on Peru for zinc and Bolivia for tin. Chile supplies us with copper. Illinois relies on the Middle East and South America for almost half its oil needs.

Here are some connections you've made yourself. These companies are multinational companies like CPC. But they are run by people in other countries. You've probably used their products.

Scripto	**Magnavox**	**Shell Oil**
Libby	**Timex**	**Sony**
Good Humor	**Volvo**	**Honda**
Keebler	**Pepsodent**	**Nestle**

In closing

It has been over 300 years since Marquette and Jolliet explored the Illinois country. Many things have changed. One thing has not. People want Illinois to stay a good place to live and work. This is your challenge. Now you know the Illinois story. You know how Illinois became a great state. Now you can help keep it great.

DO YOU REMEMBER?

Words worth remembering

Match the word from this chapter with its meaning.

1. barge
2. custom
3. export
4. buyers
5. multinational company

A. a practice regularly done by a person or persons.
B. carries goods on a river.
C. business with plants in another country.
D. to send goods out of the country in which they are made.
E. people who select goods to be sold in a store.

Ideas to remember

Find the ending that does *not* complete the sentence correctly.

6. Illinoisans are (A. all the same, B. connected to other people through customs, C. able to buy things made in other countries).
7. Missionaries (A. came to Illinois from France long ago, B. come from Illinois, C. no longer work in the world).
8. We can fly to France (A. with goods made in Illinois, B. from O'Hare Airport, C. but not from any airport in Illinois).

9. Illinois exports (A. bananas, B. soybeans, C. corn).
10. In Illinois we cannot grow (A. corn, B. cocoa beans, C. coffee beans).
11. Immigrants (A. came to Illinois for a better life, B. brought their customs with them, C. no longer come to Illinois).
12. Corn is used in making (A. soybeans, B. chewing gum, C. ice cream).
13. Multinational companies (A. are not found in Illinois, B. have plants in other countries, C. sell things in Illinois).
14. Illinois would not be a good place for (A. vacationers, B. coffee bean pickers, C. musicians).
15. Illinois became an important manufacturing giant because (A. of lakes, railroads, and rivers, B. of nearby raw materials, C. it had no entrepreneurs).

Think about it

At one time or another, someone from your family came to the United States from another place. Who were the first members of your family to come to this country? Why did they come? What customs do your family practice which had their start in another land?

Find out

Many products are made from Illinois farm products. You know about some of those which come from corn. Find out what products come from one of these Illinois agricultural products:

soybeans   hogs   cattle   wheat

In your neighborhood

Survey the telephone book for your area to find restaurants which prepare foods from other countries. Make a list of the ones you find. Then prepare a menu for your own restaurant. Show foods you enjoy and think others would visit your restaurant to eat.

DOWNTOWN CHICAGO

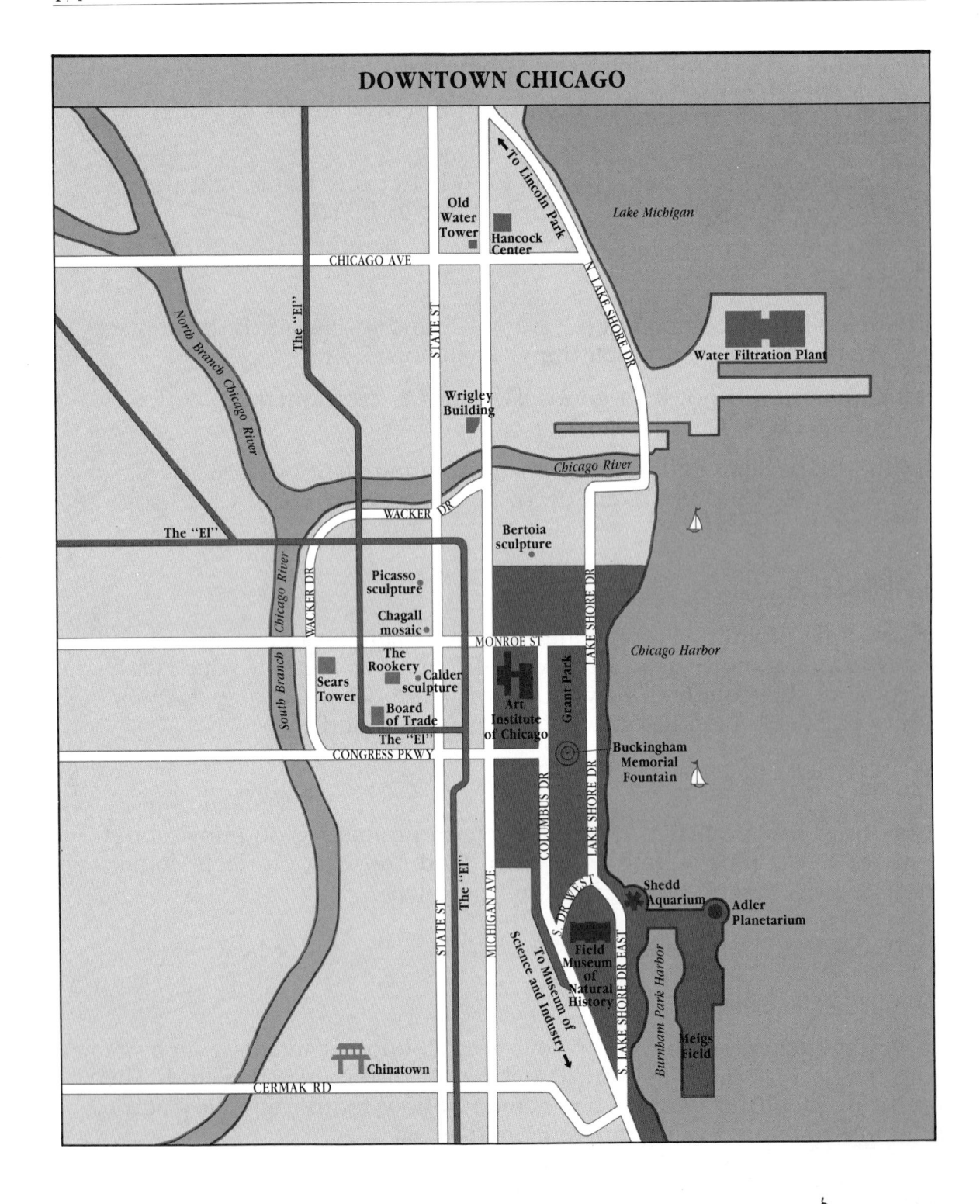

COUNTIES AND COUNTY SEATS

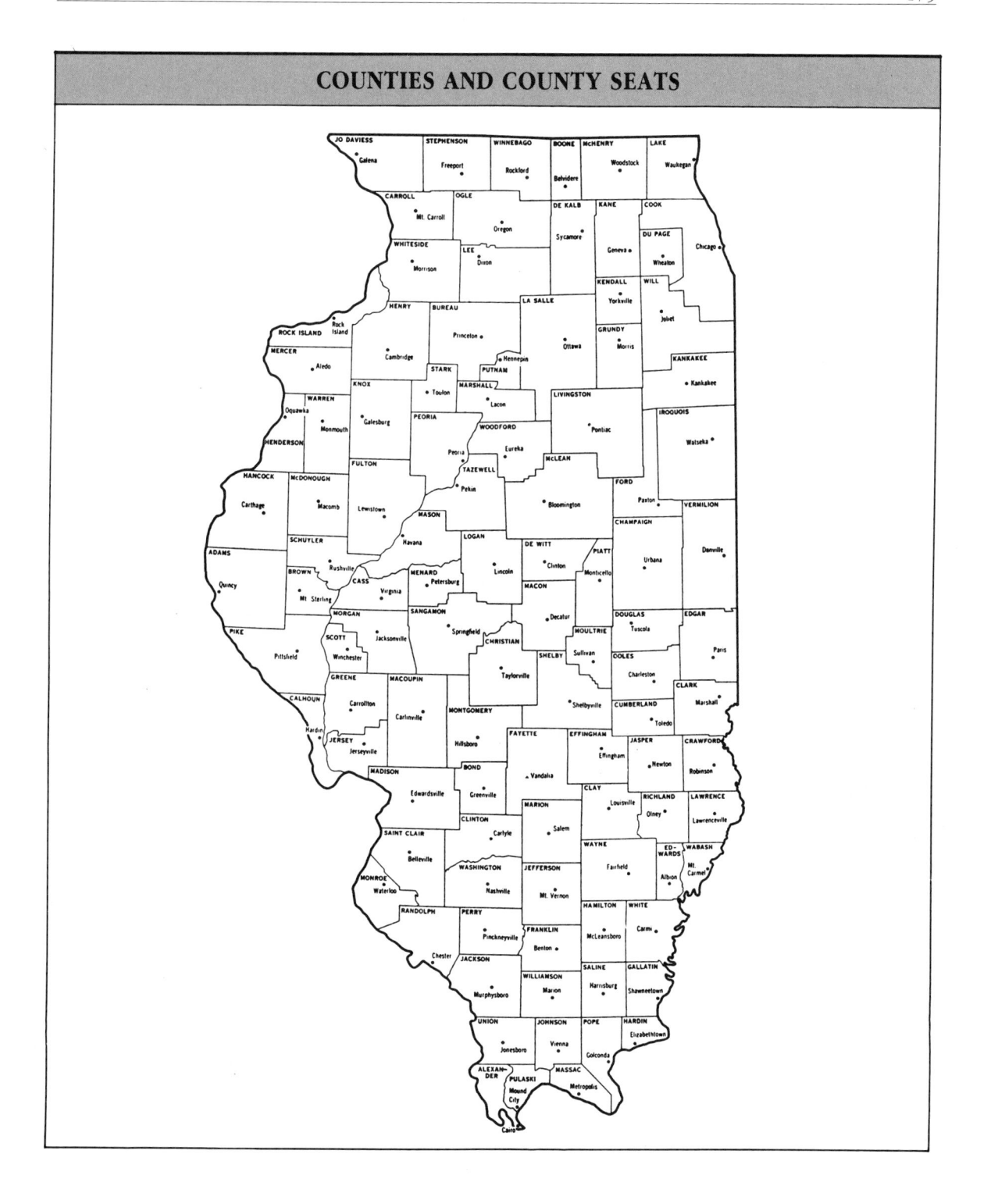

GLOSSARY

abolitionist (a-bo-LISH-un-ist) person who worked to bring an end to slavery

acrobats performers who do tumbling and jumping routines

agribusiness (AG-rih-biz-nus) the combination of all activities needed to raise and sell farm products

alliance (uh-LY-uns) group of people who agree to work together for a goal that is important to all its members

amendment a change made to a law or constitution

archeologist (ar-kee-AHL-uh-jist) a scientist who discovers how people lived long ago by searching for and studying things they left behind

architect (AR-kih-tekt) a person who designs and draws plans for a building

automation using computer-controlled machines to make things

barrack building for housing soldiers

bill written idea for a law

blacksmith one who makes horseshoes and other things from iron

bond an agreement by a government or business to pay back borrowed money

capital money, tools, or equipment used to produce goods or services; a center of government

capitol the building where state or national government officials meet to make laws

cargo the load of things on an airplane or boat

census (SEN-sus) an official count of people

city council group of people chosen to make a city's laws

coal a dark, rocklike mineral that can be burned as fuel to make heat

colony people who settle in a new land but continue to be ruled by the government at home

commander leader of a military post or group

competition a contest between two or more persons or businesses for the same thing, such as stores competing for the same customers

conductor a person who helped slaves escape on the Underground Railroad

constitution a written plan for government

construction method of building

consumer goods things to be used by individuals or households

continent (KAHN-tih-nent) one of the seven great land masses on the earth

convention a meeting for a special purpose

county an area of local government which usually includes more than one town, city, or village

court place where trials are held to settle arguments

craftsman (KRAFTS-mun) a person who is highly skilled in a certain kind of work

credit a plan for buying or using something now and paying for it some time later

crib a building in a lake used to collect drinking water for a reservoir or pumping station on land

crime an act which is against the law

debate a formal argument

declare to state something briefly and openly

depression (dee-PRESH-un) a time of low business activity and high unemployment

dextrose (DEKS-tros) a sugarlike substance gotten from starch

draft to choose people to do something

drought (DRAOWT) a very dry time when lack of rain makes growing crops hard or even impossible

editor one who prepares written works for publication

elect to choose by a vote

Emancipation Proclamation a written statement by President Lincoln announcing that slaves in Confederate states were free

empire a number of countries ruled by one country

entrepreneur (ON-truh-pruh-NOOR) a person who faces the risks of owning a business

ethnic group a group of people who are alike because of race, religion, or history

executive (egs-EK-yew-tiv) having the power and duty to carry out laws

exhibit (eg-ZIB-ut) something set out for viewing; a display

extreme (eks-TREEM) at a very high or very low degree

factors of production conditions needed to start or run a successful business

fad something popular for a short time

famine (FAM-in) an extreme lack of food

flatboat boat with a flat bottom used to float cargoes down a river

free state a state in our country with laws that did not allow slavery

gentry (JEN-tree) upper class of people

glacier (GLAI-shur) ice formed when more snow falls than melts over a period of time

goods things for sale

grain elevator a tall building used for storing grain

grassland an area with few trees where the soil is covered with grass

habitants (HAB-ih-tunts) French settlers not belonging to the upper class

homespun cloth made at home

hominy ground corn

immigrant (IM-ih-grunt) person who moves into a country from another country to live

income money received

independence freedom to govern oneself without control by others

independent free from another's control

inhabited (in-HAB-ih-tud) lived in

judicial (jew-DISH-uhl) having to do with courts and judges

jury a group of people who listen to and decide a case in court

labor work in the production of a good or service

landlord the owner of a building who rents space to others

lantern a light that can be carried

latitude (LA-tih-tood) distance north or south of the equator

laws the rules made by a government

legend (LEH-jund) an old story that is widely thought to be true but cannot be proved so

legislative (LEG-is-lai-tiv) having to do with the branch of government that makes laws

legislator (LEG-is-lai-tor) person having the legal power to make laws

legislature (LEG-is-lai-chur) part of the government that makes laws

liquor (LIH-ker) a beverage that has a high amount of alcohol

local relating to a particular place, as a town, city, or county

majority a number larger than half the total

manufacturing (man-uh-FAK-cher-eeng) making things on a large scale with the help of machinery

melting pot a term which describes the blending of different cultures

mineral a natural substance for human use taken usually from the ground

mission a church set up by a religious group to teach their beliefs to people in another area

mouth where a river empties into a lake or ocean

multinational (mul-tee-NA-shun-uhl) having plants or offices in more than one country

municipality (mew-nih-sih-PAL-ih-tee) a town, village, or city that has its own government

nation a large group of people living under the same government; a country

natural resource something that humans can use found naturally in the land, sea, or air

neutral (NOO-trul) not taking one side or another in an argument

orchestra (OR-kes-truh) a group of performers playing a number of musical instruments together

ordinance (OR-dih-nuns) a law passed by a municipality

overseer man hired to watch over the work of slaves or other workers

pantaloons (PANT-uh-loons) tight pants fastened near the ankle or strapped under the boot

pardon to excuse from being punished

patent (PA-tunt) a right given by a government to an inventor to control who uses his or her invention

pitch a black, sticky material used for roofing or paving

plank road roads made of planks nailed to trees laid across muddy areas

plantation a large farm in a warm area where workers grow sugar, cotton, rice, or tobacco

prairie early French explorers used this word, which means meadow

precipitation (pree-sip-ih-TAI-shun) rain, snow, or sleet

processing (PRAH-ses-eeng) to change a live animal into meat for the table, leather for clothing, fat for fuel and soap making, hair for brushes, etc.

profit money left when the cost of doing business is subtracted from the amount of money taken in

radar (RAI-dar) a device using radio signals to find objects

ration (RA-shun or RAI-shun) to give out in small amounts to keep from using up

re-election winning or running for the same office a second time

reaper a machine for harvesting grain

recruiter (ree-KREW-ter) one who tries to get others to agree to do a certain job

reformer one who works to improve living and working conditions

research the study of something to discover more about it

reservation (rez-er-VAI-shun) land set aside for a special use

reservoir (REZ-er-vwahr) a place where something is collected and stored; usually a pond or lake where water is stored for later use

rights powers or privileges

rival (RY-vul) one who competes with, or tries to get the same thing as, someone else

senator a person elected to help make laws

service work that helps others

sewer underground pipe or drain used to carry away waste

slum a crowded part of a city where living conditions are very poor

specialize (SPESH-uhl-ize) to limit one's energy to one business or product

speculator (SPEK-yew-lai-ter) one who risks money or something of value in the hopes of making more money

starch a substance from plants used to stiffen fabrics

station home on the Underground Railroad where people could hide

stock piece of paper that shows part ownership of a company

strike to stop work until certain demands are met

Jazz, 109
Jefferson, Thomas, 48, 53
Jenney, William LeBaron, 91, 97
Jews, 31
Joliet, 107
Jolliet, Louis, 26, 39, 172
Jonesboro, 69
Kampsville, 20
Kankakee, 28, 112
Kaskaskia, 26, 41, 42, 47, 53, 56, 120
Kaskaskia Indians, 24, 26
Kentucky, 47, 49, 70, 76, 138
Kickapoo Indians, *21*, 23
Kinzie, John, 50, 52
Kittihawa, 27
Korean War, 113
Koster Site, *20*
LaSalle, 24, 162
LaSalle, Robert Cavalier de, 38-40
Lake Calumet, 147
Lake Michigan, 6, 28, 50, 54, 84, 86, 87, 90, 102, 127, 147
Lake Peoria, 40
Lake Superior, 18, 20
Land values, 85, 96
Laotians, 32
Law, how a bill becomes, 123-125, *124*
Lead, 44, 45
Legends, 29, 92
Lincoln, Abraham, 55, 70-80, 121, 161, 162; childhood, 70-71; debates with Douglas, 69, 73; elected president, 63, 70, 79
Lincoln, Mary Todd, 73
Lincoln, Nancy, 70
Lincoln, Sarah, 70
Lincoln, Thomas, 70
Lincoln-Douglas debates, 69, 73
Lisle, 162
Lockport, 102
Lovejoy, Elijah, 59-60, 67-68
Lovejoy, Owen, 67-68
Mail-order buying, 103-105, *104*, 149
Marquette, Father Jacques, 26, 38-39, 172
May, Harvey Henry, 57
McCormick, Cyrus Hall, 57, 58, 84, 143, 144-145
Meat-packing 84, 91, 145, 146
Melting pot, 32
Meredosia, 88
Mexicans, 31, 32
Michegamea Indians, 24
Minerals, 45, 138-139, 171
Mining, 28, 31, 44, 45, 120, 138-140, *138, 140*
Missions, 26, 41, 160
Mississippi River, 26, 30, 39, 40, 43, 46, 49, 55, 56, *166*, 167
Mississippian Period, 17, 18-20, 21
Missouri, 30, 59, 76
Moingwena Indians, 24
Moline, 29, 57, 107, 144, 165
Moody, Dwight L., 100, *101*
Mormons, 30, 162

Mound Builders, 17, 18-20, *18, 19, 20*, 21
Movies, 109
Mueller, Hieronymous A., 108
Multinational companies, 167-168, 171
Museum of Science and Industry, 98, 162
Nagasaki, Japan, 152
Natural resources, 136-137, 138-139, 147
Nauvoo, 30, 162
New Deal, 112
New Orleans, 27, 41, 42, 45, 46, 63, 71, 72, 112, 167
New Salem, 72, 73, 131, 161, 162
New York, 24, 30, 40, 57
North Chicago, 167
Northbrook, 167
Northwest Territory, 51, 53
O'Hare Airport, *166*, 167
Oak Brook, 153
Ohio River, 47, 49
Olmsted, Frederick, 91
Ottawa, 24, 26, 69
Palmer House, 95
Palmer, Potter, 95, 103
Pana, 141
Parrish, George I., Jr., 90
Pearl Harbor, Hawaii, 110
Peoria, 26, 39, 88, 107, 112, 142, 165
Peoria Indians, 24
Petersburg, 162
Poles, 31
Pope, Nathaniel, 54
Potawatomi Indians, 27, 55, 127
Prairie, 5, *5*, 21, 57, 113
Prairie du Rocher, 26
President, 118, 119, 142, 148
Prophetstown, 55
Pullman, 147-148
Pullman Palace Car Company, 147
Pullman strike 148, *148*
Pullman, George, 147-148
Quincy, 69, 88
Race riots, 107
Radar, 112
Radio, 109, 111, 153
Railroads, 10, 31, 58-59, 66, 78, 87-91, 105, 139, 142, 145, 147, 165
Rally Round the Flag, 67, 75
Rantoul, 106
Reaper, 57, 58, *58*, 66, 144
Reformers, 100
Refrigerator, 109, 139
Religion, 18, 26, 28, 29, 30, 38, 119, 158, 160-161
Renault, Philippe, 45
Revolutionary War, *see* American Revolution
Riverside, 91
Rock Island, 55, 88, 107, 112
Rockford, 106, 107, 112
Romanians, 31
Roosevelt, Franklin, 110
Root, George F., 75

Russians, 31
Salt, 138-139, 140
Sanitary and Ship Canal, 102
Sauk Indians, 55, *56*, 127
Schaumburg, 167
Sears, Richard, 103-105
Selkirk, Dr. James, 108
Senate, state, 123, 124, 125
Senate, U.S., 119
Service industries, 149-151, *150*
Settlement houses, 33, 101, 102, *102*
Skyscrapers, 31, 97, 126
Slavery, 27-28, 31, 45, 59-60, 63, 64-69, *65*, 70, 73, 74, 76, 78
Sleeping car, 147
Slums, 100, 102
Smith, Hyrum, 30
Smith, Joseph, 30, *30*
Soybeans, 6, 112, 145, 169
Sports, 109, 163
Springfield, 53, 88, 112, 121, 122, 131, 138, 161, 162
St. Charles, 117, 127
St. Lawrence River, 39, 167
St. Louis, Missouri, 59
Starr, Ellen Gates, 102
Starved Rock, 24, 40, 162
Statehood, 28, 53
Steel-making, 31, 147, 165
Stock market crash, 109, 110, 111
Suburbs, 108
Swedish, 29, 31, 161
Tamoroa Indians, 24
Taxes, 107, 121, 126, 130-131
Technology, 151-154
Telegraph, 94
Television, *135*, 157
Tonti, Henri de, 38-40
Trade, 17-18, 20, 21, 26-27, 28, 38, 39, 41, 50, 84, 137
Transportation, 5, 10, 42, 57, 58, 78, 84, 98, 127, 165-167, *166*
Trolley, 31, 96
Truman, Harry, 152
Tubman, Harriet, 68
Twenties, 109
Underground Railroad, 67, *68*
Union Stock Yards, 91, 146
Unions, 141-143
United States Constitution, *see* Constitution, U.S.
University of Chicago, 152-153
Utica, 39
Vandalia, 53, 56, 57, 73, 121, *121*
Victory gardens, 113
Vietnam War, 113
Vietnamese, 32
Vincennes, Indiana, 47
Virden, 141, *142*
Virginia, 47, 49, 57, 76, 144
Wabash, 49, *49*
War of 1812, 52, 53
Ward, Aaron Montgomery, 103-105
Washington, D.C., 54, 57, 80, 110, 118
Wheat, 6, 42, 58, 78, 91, 169

183

Wheaton, 162
White House, 118
Women, in Civil War, 75, 76; in WWI, 106; in WWII, 113
Woodland Indians, 21-24
World War I, 105-107, 109, 111
World War II, 110, 152
World's fair, *see* Columbian Exposition
Yates, Richard, 76
YMCA, 100